COMPUTER SCIENCE, TECHNOLOGY AND APPLICATIONS

A CLOSER LOOK AT CYBERSECURITY AND CRYPTANALYSIS

COMPUTER SCIENCE, TECHNOLOGY AND APPLICATIONS

Additional books and e-books in this series can be found on Nova's website under the Series tab.

COMPUTER SCIENCE, TECHNOLOGY AND APPLICATIONS

A CLOSER LOOK AT CYBERSECURITY AND CRYPTANALYSIS

CH. RUPA

AND

MOHAMMAD SIRAJUDDIN

EDITORS

Copyright © 2020 by Nova Science Publishers, Inc.

All rights reserved. No part of this book may be reproduced, stored in a retrieval system or transmitted in any form or by any means: electronic, electrostatic, magnetic, tape, mechanical photocopying, recording or otherwise without the written permission of the Publisher.

We have partnered with Copyright Clearance Center to make it easy for you to obtain permissions to reuse content from this publication. Simply navigate to this publication's page on Nova's website and locate the "Get Permission" button below the title description. This button is linked directly to the title's permission page on copyright.com. Alternatively, you can visit copyright.com and search by title, ISBN, or ISSN.

For further questions about using the service on copyright.com, please contact:
Copyright Clearance Center
Phone: +1-(978) 750-8400   Fax: +1-(978) 750-4470   E-mail: info@copyright.com.

NOTICE TO THE READER

The Publisher has taken reasonable care in the preparation of this book, but makes no expressed or implied warranty of any kind and assumes no responsibility for any errors or omissions. No liability is assumed for incidental or consequential damages in connection with or arising out of information contained in this book. The Publisher shall not be liable for any special, consequential, or exemplary damages resulting, in whole or in part, from the readers' use of, or reliance upon, this material. Any parts of this book based on government reports are so indicated and copyright is claimed for those parts to the extent applicable to compilations of such works.

Independent verification should be sought for any data, advice or recommendations contained in this book. In addition, no responsibility is assumed by the Publisher for any injury and/or damage to persons or property arising from any methods, products, instructions, ideas or otherwise contained in this publication.

This publication is designed to provide accurate and authoritative information with regard to the subject matter covered herein. It is sold with the clear understanding that the Publisher is not engaged in rendering legal or any other professional services. If legal or any other expert assistance is required, the services of a competent person should be sought. FROM A DECLARATION OF PARTICIPANTS JOINTLY ADOPTED BY A COMMITTEE OF THE AMERICAN BAR ASSOCIATION AND A COMMITTEE OF PUBLISHERS.

Additional color graphics may be available in the e-book version of this book.

Library of Congress Cataloging-in-Publication Data

ISBN: 978-1-53618-165-4

Published by Nova Science Publishers, Inc. † New York

Contents

Preface		vii
Acknowledgments		ix
Chapter 1	Cryptanalysis from an Adversary View: A Detailed Analogy of Cryptanalysis *Karthik Sainadh Siddabattula*	1
Chapter 2	Cryptanalysis and Various Attacks *Meerjavali Shaik*	9
Chapter 3	Evolution of Cryptanalysis Techniques: A Review *Mohammad Sirajuddin and Ande Prasad*	21
Chapter 4	Role of Penetration Testing in Security Analysis *Ch. Rupa*	35
Chapter 5	Vulnerability Assessment Using Nessus Tool *Ch. Rupa*	49
Chapter 6	Digitization with Cyber Security and AI: A Review *S. Gopi Krishna, Mohammd Sirajuddin and S. Suresh Babu*	63

Chapter 7	An Analytical Approach for Checking the Performance of Different Classifiers in Network of IDS *N. Raghavendra Sai*	**73**
Chapter 8	Smart IoT Device for Women Safety *Chattu Padmini, Gade Brahma Reddy, Kunapareddy Chaitanya Sai, Chundru Sowmya Lalitha and Bode Siri Krishna*	**89**
About the Editors		**99**
Index		**101**

PREFACE

This book entitled *"A Closer Look at Cryptanalysis"* focuses on the fundamental concepts of cryptanalysis and various types of security attacks. Also gives detail discussion on role of cryptanalysis in identifying the vulnerabilities and related tools to perform cryptanalysis.

It holds role of penetration testing which is required for security analysis as well as vulnerability assessment. Usage of one of real time tools for penetration testing is explained. This kind of illustration helps reader to learn the concepts practically. Moreover, evolution of cryptanalysis process also discussed in this book as a chapter.

This book contains chapters that explains the importance of emerging technologies in ensuring security. Usage of Data mining techniques in Intrusion Detection System (IDS), role of AI in securing digital world and a practical application for ensuring security based on IoT are explained precisely.

This book will give reader an exhaustive idea with practical applications in the context of security and cryptanalysis.

Target Audience
- UG/PG Students
- Instructors
- Research Scholars

ACKNOWLEDGMENTS

First and foremost we covey special thanks to Nova Publishers for giving us an opportunity to come up with this book.

We are grateful for the valuable contributions made by the following individuals for shaping this book.

Dr. S. Gopi Krishna, Professor, Sri Mittapalli College of Engineering, Guntur, India.

Dr. Ande Prasad, Professor, Vikrama Simhapuri University, Nellore, India.

Mr. S. Suresh Babu, Associate Professor, Sri Mittapalli College of Engineering, Guntur, India.

Dr. N. Raghavendra Sai, Professor, Koneru Lakshmaiah Education Fundation, Guntur, India.

Mrs. Padmini Chattu, Assistant Professor, Dhanekula Institute of Engineering & Technology, Vijayawada, India.

Karthik Sainadh Siddabattula, VR Siddhartha Engineering College, India.

Meerjavali. Shaik, VR Siddhartha Engineering College, India.

Gade Brahma Reddy, Dhanekula Institute of Engineering & Technology, Vijayawada, India.

Kunapareddy Chaitanya Sai, Dhanekula Institute of Engineering & Technology, Vijayawada, India

Chundru Sowmyalalitha, Dhanekula Institute of Engineering & Technology, Vijayawada, India.

Bode Siri Krishna, Dhanekula Institute of Engineering & Technology, Vijayawada, India.

We also thank all the reviewers for giving valuable suggestions and feedback for improving the quality of this book.

Last, but not least, we thank all our family members, friends, and colleagues for supporting us throughout the writing of this book.

Ch. Rupa
and
MD. Sirajuddin
Editors

In: A Closer Look at Cybersecurity ...　ISBN: 978-1-53618-165-4
Editors: Ch. Rupa et al.　© 2020 Nova Science Publishers, Inc.

Chapter 1

CRYPTANALYSIS FROM AN ADVERSARY VIEW: A DETAILED ANALOGY OF CRYPTANALYSIS

Karthik Sainadh Siddabattula[*]
Department of CSE, VR Siddhartha Engineering College,
Vijayawada, Andhra Pradesh, India

ABSTRACT

Even today, the cryptographers strive to develop ciphers that encrypt sensitive data to furnish privacy for users. The developed ciphers yield an unreadable format of data, which we termed it as Ciphertext. This Ciphertext generated is most reliable if the cipher used to encrypt is a flawless cipher. To determine whether a cipher is vulnerable or not, we use a technique known as cryptanalysis. The cause for the birth of numerous ciphers is successful cryptanalysis. The cryptanalysis is a process of detailed examination and analysis of a cipher from an adversary view. An adversary is the one who attacks the cryptographic

---

[*] Corresponding Author's Email: sainadhkarthik7143@gmail.com.

algorithm to recover plain text. In this chapter, we perform some known cryptanalysis techniques.

Keywords: cryptanalysis, adversary, cryptology, cryptanalyst

INTRODUCTION

Protecting information systems is the most prominent aspect to be considered. No matter what the information is. It might be a name, phone number, password, payment card details; every piece of information needs a wrapper that protects it from evil eyes. As we already know, cryptology, often called cryptography, achieves the protection by sending the plain text into robust ciphers, which performs data encryption, resulting in a ciphertext. The additional parameter used to encrypt the plaintext is the secret key. This key may vary in size, depending on the algorithm. Some algorithms may use the same key for both encryption and decryption. Other algorithms may use different keys for encryption and decryption, but somehow both the keys are related. The entire cryptanalysis revolves around on how to recover the plain text or to gain the key. Cryptanalyst won't concern about how robust the cipher is, the only goal is to construct the plain text from the Ciphertext. The term cryptanalysis often defined as a study of investigating cryptographic algorithms to discover the flaws in cipher that may give you access to the content of encrypted information without knowing the secret key. In the rest of this chapter, we'll see:

- What parameters do we need to consider to do cryptanalysis?
- Where the cryptanalysis takes place?
- And much more.

METHODS

What Parameters Do We Need to Consider for Cryptanalysis?

The success rate of cryptanalysis highly depends on how secure the cipher is? And also what parameters we have considered. If the cipher was weak, then analysis can be done quickly. The parameters we choose must be in such a way that those should yield a secret key or the plain text. Some ciphers need simple standard parameters, but whereas some other ciphers need complex, uncommon parameters. So it depends on what cipher we have chosen for cryptanalysis. The core parameters that can make cryptanalysis is the ciphertext and encryption algorithm. To make our analysis successful, we need to have these two parameters in our hands. In earlier chapters, we have already discussed some standard parameters.

Let us recall them for our walkthrough of Affine cipher.

Ciphertext only: In this consideration, we have the only Ciphertext with the encryption algorithm known.

Known plaintext: We have plaintext – ciphertext pair constructed with the secret key.

Chosen plaintext: Cryptanalyst selects plaintext, in the presence of a secret key, the framing of Ciphertext occurs.

Chosen Ciphertext: Ciphertext is taken by the analyst, which stated to be true along with its corresponding decrypted plain text constructed with the key.

Chosen text: This is a combination of both 'chosen-plaintext' and 'chosen-ciphertext.'

In the next section, we see where the cryptanalysis takes place? At the end of this chapter, we cryptanalysis the infamous substitution cipher known as Affine Cipher.

Where the Cryptanalysis Takes Place?

As we already discussed, the cryptanalyst intends to recover the plain text or to yield a key that decrypts the Ciphertext. If the latter case gets existed, then it can be a menace. As a result of successful cryptanalysis concerning key retrieval, future conversations are prone to decryption by using the key gained.

Let us take a legacy example where Jessy wants to send a specific message to Jenny, as shown in Figure 1. The typical communication channel has the capability of transmitting a message from the sender (Jessy) to the receiver (Jenny). The entire communication had shown in Figure 1.

As illustrated in Figure 1, a message is getting transmitted to Jenny from Jessy. Now the cryptanalyst, John, steps into the communication channel to yield Ciphertext into his evil hands. In most cases, the encryption algorithm said to be admitted by the cryptanalyst. And then, the cryptanalysis gets started with other necessary parameters. In simple words, the cryptanalysis takes place between the communication of two parties.

In further sections, we are going to see how to break down Affine cipher? And what made the Affine cipher to be weak in terms of confidentiality.

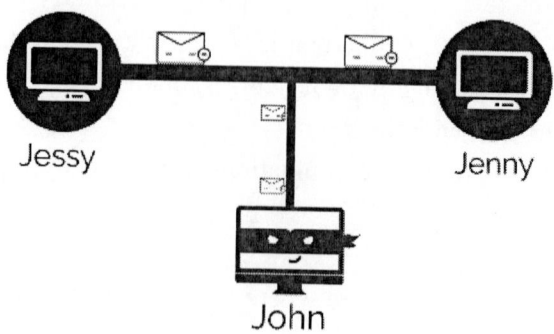

Figure 1. Venue of cryptanalysis.

How Affine Cipher Works?

Affine cipher falls under the breed of the monoalphabetic cipher. Monoalphabetic ciphers are the ones in which we portray the letters of plaintext to its corresponding numerical values. The numerical values are enciphered using an encipherment algorithm and mapped back to the respective alphabet to form the Ciphertext. The reason for Affine cipher of being special is it employs two keys. By using the two secret keys, plaintext's numerical values get encrypted, and Ciphertext numerical values get decrypted.

Let's drive into practical on how to achieve confidentiality by taking two secret keys with Affine cipher:

We represent the first key as 'a,' and its value must be anyone among 1, 3, 5, 7, 9, 11, 15, 17, 19, 21, 23, 25. And denotation of the second key is as 'b,' and its value can be anyone ranging from 0 to 25.

Concerning secret keys generated, the encipherment will be as follows:

$$C = (a * p + b) \bmod 26$$

And its corresponding decipherment will be:

$$P = a^{-1}(c - b) \bmod 26$$

a^{-1} represents the modular multiplicative inverse of 'a.'

Now let us consider an example where the plaintext is "CRYPT."

C	R	Y	P	T – plaintext
2	17	24	15	19 - corresponding numerical values.

Choose the keypair. We take 'a' as 15. And 'b' as 19.
The encipherment will be as follows:

$(15 * 2 + 19) \, mod \, 26 = 23$

$(15 * 17 + 19) \, mod \, 26 = 14$

$(15 * 24 + 19) \, mod \, 26 = 15$

$(15 * 15 + 19) \, mod \, 26 = 10$

$(15 * 19 + 19) \, mod \, 26 = 18$

Ciphertext is shown below:

23 14   15   10   18 - numericals generated
X   O   P   K   S - ciphertext.

"XOPKS" is then transmitted to thereceiver. There the decipherment is done as shown below:

X   O   P   K   S - ciphertext
23 14   15   10   18 - corresponding numerical values.

Now we have to calculate the modular multiplicative inverse of 'a.' Let's take an online resource to find it.
We get the modular multiplicative inverse of a (15) is 7.
The decipherment is as follows:

7(23-19) mod 26 = 2

7(14-19) mod 26 = 17

$7(15-19) \mod 26 = 24$

$7(10-19) \mod 26 = 15$

$7(18-19) \mod 26 = 19$

Plain text recovered is as follows:

2	17	24	15	19 - numericals generated
C	R	Y	P	T - plain text recovered.

The Weakness of Affine Cipher

The number of possible keys for the first key is 12. And for the second key is 26. So the possible keypairs are $12 * 26 = 312$. For a standard computer, the key pick becomes much easy(Brute force). If we assume the message we encrypted is in the language English, then the total number of letters are 26. In Affine cipher, the first key must be relatively coprime to 26. Unfortunately, this makes only 12 quantity of numbers are available as coprime to 26. So, therefore, 312 keypairs are not much high range to try for a plaintext recovery. If the cryptanalyst can discover the plaintext by employing brute force technique or guessing intellectually then, the Affine cipher gets to blow off. Due to this, the Affine cipher became a vulnerable monoalphabetic cipher.

Cryptanalysis of Affine Cipher

In the previous section, we have seen what made the Affine cipher weaker. Let us admit it and take a step forward to cryptanalysis the Affine cipher.

Table 1. Cryptanalysis of Affine Cipher

(x, b)	Plain text recovered
(1,1)	W N O I R
(5,6)	H O T U I
(7,19)	C R Y P T
(15,20)	X O D G W
(11,19)	S X I F P

Here, we apply some random keypairs to recover plain text. Finally, we check among the retrieved text for desired plain text, merely guessing one of them.

Consider the previous example "XOPKS," the Ciphertext of "CRYPT."

We take keypairs in the form: (x, b). Here, 'x' is the modular multiplicative inverse of 'a,' where 'a' is the one among the 12 coprime numbers of 26. 'b' is taken as usual as we took in the previous section.

The cryptanalysis has given in Table 1, which provides you with a better understanding.

By seeing the above plaintexts, we can simply summarize the 3rd try gave the desired result. The reason we have chosen the 3rd try is that other keypairs had failed to provide a better English semantics, whereas (7, 19) keypair gave at its best.

By the above studies, we can say how easy it is to break down the Affine cipher.

CONCLUSION

Every cipher is vulnerable, but not yet discovered. The objective of cryptanalysis is to state that it provides a way to assess the weakness of a cipher. The parameters consideration may vary from cipher to cipher; however, it grabs a vast knowledge to discover the vulnerability. Although Affine cipher is not fit for our today's daily life encryption mechanisms, it stood at the best grade for the sake of demonstrating semantic cryptanalysis like what we have discussed in this chapter.

In: A Closer Look at Cybersecurity …
Editors: Ch. Rupa et al.
ISBN: 978-1-53618-165-4
© 2020 Nova Science Publishers, Inc.

Chapter 2

CRYPTANALYSIS AND VARIOUS ATTACKS

Meerjavali Shaik
Department of Computer Science, VR Siddhartha,
Kanuru, Vijayawada, AP, India

ABSTRACT

For most of the Cryptographic algorithms that are developed or being developed at present, the prime problem being faced is vulnerability.

There is not an algorithm or a system which can stand without proning to an attack because everything has vulnerabilities and/or glitches.

Cryptanalysis[1] is the considered solution to make the algorithm run by finding, reducing the chance of vulnerabilities; on the other hand, it is a useful weapon for attackers to attack the system. In this chapter, I would like to explain the birth of cryptanalysis and various cryptanalysis techniques.

Keywords: Cryptography [10], vulnerability, glitch, cryptanalysis [1].

INTRODUCTION

We know that analysis means the detailed examination of elements or structure of something and cryptography [10] means the method of protecting information using codes, where 'crypt' means hidden and 'graphy' means writing. Hence, we write codes to hide the information using cryptography [10]. Cryptanalysis [1] is the process of finding the hidden meaning present in the attained data through a deep examination of the codes.

Cryptanalysis came into existence and was publicly acknowledged in the year 1990 by Murphy. He is recognized for his efforts in cryptanalysis of a block cipher called FEAL. It is developed by Akihiro Shimizu and shoji miyaguchi from NTT in the year 1987. Initially, FEAL [10] cipher stood as an alternative algorithm for DES [10]. Murphy found FEAL cipher to be susceptible to various forms of cryptanalysis [1] and it lead the path to discovering linear and differential cryptanalysis on various block ciphers. At present, both block ciphers and stream ciphers like salsa20 [4], chacha, also face cryptanalysis attacks.

Cryptanalysis [1] also includes passive attacks on premises/ property. Passive attacks include eavesdropping on, monitoring of, and transmissions. Passive attacks are divided into two types; one is the release of message contents and the other is traffic analysis. In both the cases, the message is unaltered and encrypted; allowing for a possible attacker to make out patterns by observing. Cryptanalysis is used in informative warfare applications e.g., decoding the ciphertext without the use of a key.

According to Diffie and Hellman [5], "skill in the production of cryptanalysis has always been heavy on the side of the professionals, but innovation, particularly in the design of new types of cryptographic systems, has come primarily from amateurs". Thus, every system is designed with a bug in it.

METHODS

There are a bunch of methods explained below demonstrating cryptanalysis techniques to attack a designed/developed algorithm using a block cipher, a stream cipher, and hashing algorithms.

Ciphertext Only Attack

In this case, the encrypted message is available to the atacker; he can use this encrypted message to study and observe patterns and decode the attained results to the original message.

For example consider a message 'ih' is encrypted as 'hi', similarly 'eyb' as "bye". Therefore attacker by observing the patterns can definitely can solve the puzzle and attack the system.

Known Plaintext Attack

In this case, attackers know or can guess the original plaintext from ciphertext generated by the algorithm which allows him to determine the key.

For example some systems run on xor cipher i.e., plaintext xor with key gives cipher text. Therefore if attackers knows the cipher text, plaintext by xor cipher he will determine the key.

Chosen Plaintext Attack

In this case, the attacker is acknowledged with some plaintext. He observes the trends in the ciphertext to determine the design of the system, leading way to key generation.

For example let us consider the plaintext is 'good morning jack, have a good day' it is encrypted as 'work daily then, your work stress reduces'. The plain text has repeated good two times similarly the cipher text repeated work two times thus it weakens the system security.

Chosen Ciphertext Attack

In this case, the attacker will make a deep analysis of the traffic and capture/choose some ciphertext for which he plans to decrypt/decipher. After observing various chosen-ciphertext, he is able to trace out the key to chosen plain text.

Man-in-the-Middle Attack

In this case, parties who are communicating through a channel think it's secure but the attacker trespasses to a position which is feasible for attack as shown in the below Figure 1 alice messages can be seen, modified, and damaged by Mallory until it reaches bob.

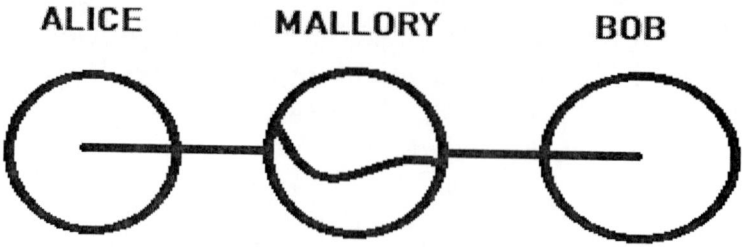

Figure 1. Man in the middle attack [7].

In this MITM [7] attack, the attacker is the middle man but both end parties are unaware of this reality and they position him as a key exchange officer between themselves. The attacker performs key exchange with each party. MITM attacks mostly on public-key cryptography.

Brute Force Attack

The primary attack on any system design is a brute force attack. It is also called a trial and error method; it is mostly used to crack the passwords, Atm Pins.

The evolution of supercomputer in the 20th century plays a major role in the deep analysis of secret codes. The table-1 shows the attacking time slabs for a given length of the key.

Table 1. Length of key vs. attack time [5]

Length of a key in bits	Possible no. of keys can be generated	Attacking time
56	7.2 * 10^6	20 hours
80	1.2 * 10^24	54,800 years
128	3.4 * 10^38	1.5 * 10^19 years
256	1.15 * 10^77	5.2 * 10^57 years

With the increase in the key length, the increase in the attack time can be concluded from the above table.

Side-Channel Attack

In this type, attacks are possible because of reverse engineering procedures.

Attackers act as an ideal person when the algorithm is working, they make note of every minute information like the details of the system in which the algorithms run, the time it has taken, and the number of electromagnetic radiations emitted, power consumption. SCA [19] are inexpensive.

Malleability Attack

During malleability [3] attack, the ciphertext is transformed into such a way that it can be deciphered into another plaintext. The target of the attacker is not determining the key; his target is to describe the failure of the cryptosystem. Even though keystream is produced by a secure system, it can also fail. The Figure 2 below describes the Malleability attack. It mostly occurs in bank cryptosystems.

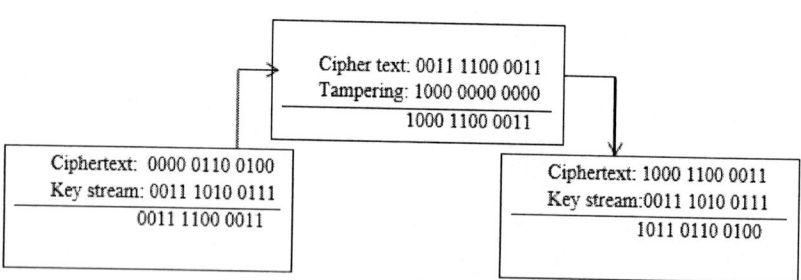

Figure 2. Describing the malleability attack [3].

Birthday Attack

All the attacks discussed above are on encryption algorithms but birthday attack is different from them, it is an attack against hashing algorithms.

We know that no two messages have the same message digest, it is a unique property of hashing algorithms. Birthday attacks say similar message digest can be extracted from two similar inputs but with not the same inputs. A strong hash function should be implemented to resist a birthday attack.

It is quiet compared to birthday name because for example consider a classroom there is a chance of two different students born on same day.

Divide and Conquer Attack

In this case, the problem is divided into smaller parts to reduce the computation problem-solving mechanism. Hence, attackers implement this method and divide ciphertext complexity. In computer science, divide and conquer algorithm is used to optimize into the smaller parts to obtain the benefits.

Correlation Attack

Correlation [3, 12] attack occurs only when there is a weakness in the ciphertext. We can identify the Secret key easily by using some mathematical interpretations. And the algorithm which is attacked by this attack is statistically biased encryption.

Guess and Determine Attack

Stream cipher has key Stream to input plain text but this attack abuses the fact that only a few internal bits are given as input to the filtered function.

Therefore, only these values determine the computed keystream bit, and consequently, there is a chance of guessing the key value by various methods like elimination, randomization, etc.

Power Analysis Attack

Power analysis is a form of attack in which the attacker observes the power consumption of cryptographic hardware. Power analysis are of two types; one is simple power analysis [19] and the other is differential power analysis [19], which is more advanced. Power analysis is an example of a side-channel attack.

Some General Cryptanalysis Attacks

Some cryptographic algorithms are complex, they include many round logics. Therefore, the attacker attends to each logic and examines every test block that is released after the round logic is to extract the original key length and key value. In some filtered function round logics, only a few input stream bits have taken part in encryption. Thus, attackers take this as an advantage to obtain the key-value and destroy the system.

RECOMMENDED STRATEGY

To overcome the cryptanalysis attacks or to counter the attacks following strategies are suggested.

1. *Chaotic encryption algorithms*: Here the algorithms are born with a state to create confusion in attackers' minds. Some chaotic [2] encryption based on image encryption mechanism, DNA encryption mechanism are used because these features are unique.
2. *Robust protocols usage*: Most of the attacks occur in transmission media. Usage of robust security protocols in

file/message transmission makes the system a bit more secure. Some robust security protocols are two-way handshake protocol [16], three-way handshake [16] protocol.

3. *Key size increment*: Increase in key length creates some complexity. Therefore, increasing the key length by exponent 2 creates more transformations. Using mathematical operations like DCT, making permutation operation creates ambiguity and makes it less prone to brute force attacks.

4. *Prevention of side-channel attacks*: Reducing the release of electromagnetic radiation by computing hardware, keeping values of time used, the power consumed and hardware used in secret can increase the life span of the cryptosystem.

5. *Digital signature usage for key exchange*: Key is an important determining factor in the cryptography system. Key exchange should be done in a more secure way. Hence the usage of digital signature gives authentication service to us because digital signature uses hashing algorithms like SHA [17], MD [18] which strongly builds systems.

6. *Multiple keys usage*: As the password/pin is strongly built-in lock, the key also has similar feature; it also locks the system. Usage of multiple keys increases the level of difficulty to attack. Suppose, consider a door closed and locked with 10 locks, it needs 10 keys namely k1, k2, k3, ..., k10 to open the door. Therefore, the thief should have stolen 10 keys to open the door, but it is a herculean task to him.

7. *Secure hardware usage*: secure hardware means strong built system design, strong procedure architecture. Still, research is going on to invent secure hardware and embedded systems. Batch files operated system is more secure than todays super computers.

CONCLUSION

Evolution of quantum computers and supercomputers encouraged cryptanalysis for fast processing because these systems use less time to predicate the key value.

Usage of algorithms like shor's [13] will factor large key numbers in polynomial time, it effects breaking some generally used forms of asymmetric key encryption.

By using grovers's [14] algorithm we can find brute-force key-value quadratically faster in a quantum computer. However, this could be countered by doubling the key length.

To prevent some of these cryptanalysis attacks we can compute a cryptographic hash of the key exchange and sign it with digital signature [15] algorithm and send it to the other side, then the receiver verifies the hash with locally computed hash to see if both hashes match and the signature came from desired other party. If they don't match, it is a masquerade attack.

Even though having various effects from cryptanalysis, it is efficient because it helps us improve our standard in making new robust algorithms.

REFERENCES

[1] Wagstaff, Samuel S. Jr., Dept. of Maths and Statistics *"Cryptanalysis of number theoretic ciphers"*, version 6, 2019, https://doi.org/10.1201/9781315275765.

[2] L. Chen, J. Chen, G. Zhao and S. Wang, "Cryptanalysis and Improvement of a Chaos-Based Watermarking Scheme," in *IEEE Access*, vol. 7, pp. 97549-97565, 2019.

[3] Roel Verdict, Institute for computing and information sciences redbud University Nijmegen, The Netherlands. *"Introduction to cryptanalysis: Attacking Stream Cipher"*.

[4] Bernstein, Daniel J. Department of mathematics, statistics, computer science, the University of Illinois at Chicago. *"The salsa20 stream of family ciphers"*.

[5] https://www.experts-exchange.com/articles/12460/Cryptanalysis-and-Attacks.html.

[6] https://en.wikipedia.org/wiki/Block_cipher.

[7] https://en.wikipedia.org/wiki/Man-in-the-middle-attack#/media/File:Man_in_the_middle_attack.svg.

[8] https://en.wikipedia.org/wiki/Cryptanalysis.

[9] https://www.rambus.com/timing-attacks-on-implementations-of-diffiehellman-rsa-dss-and-other-systems/.

[10] Stallings, William. fifth edition, *Cryptographic and Network Security Principles and Practice*, 2014.

[11] Corman, Thomas H. *"Introduction to algorithms"*.

[12] https://en.wikipedia.org/wiki/Correlation_attack.

[13] P. W. Shor, "Algorithms for quantum computation: discrete logarithms and factoring," *Proceedings 35th Annual Symposium on Foundations of Computer Science*, Santa Fe, NM, USA, 1994, pp. 124-134.

[14] Grover L. K. A fast quantum mechanical algorithm for database search, *Proceedings, 28th Annual ACM Symposium on the Theory of Computing*, (May 1996) p. 212.

[15] *Digital signature algorithm*, https://youtu.be/qFbQkSywvlQ.

[16] H. Altunbasak and H. Owen, "Alternative Pair-wise Key Exchange Protocols for Robust Security Networks (IEEE 802.11i) in Wireless LANs," *IEEE SoutheastCon*, 2004. Proceedings., Greensboro, North Carolina, USA, 2004, pp. 77-83.

[17] *Sha-512 algorithm*, https://youtube/wNBlwmJQbC8.

[18] *MD5 algorithm*, https://youtube/NdrCm-aIcPo.

[19] S. D. Putra, A. S. Ahmad and S. Sutikno, "Power analysis attack on implementation of DES," *2016 International Conference on Information Technology Systems and Innovation (ICITSI)*, Bandung, 2016, pp. 1-6.

In: A Closer Look at Cybersecurity …
Editors: Ch. Rupa et al.
ISBN: 978-1-53618-165-4
© 2020 Nova Science Publishers, Inc.

Chapter 3

EVOLUTION OF CRYPTANALYSIS TECHNIQUES: A REVIEW

Mohammad Sirajuddin[1,*] *and Ande Prasad*[2,†]

[1]Department of C.S.E, Koneru Lakshmaiah Education Foundation (KLEF), Guntur, Andhra Pradesh, India
[2]Department of C.S, Vikrama Simhapuri University, Nellore, Andhra Pradesh, India

ABSTRACT

Cryptanalysis is the process of determining the decryption scheme without the knowledge of the algorithm and the key used. This chapter brings out a discussion on the cryptanalysis of various prominent security algorithms. This chapter also describes recent cryptanalysis schemes along with future challenges. The role of advanced concepts like AI and DNA computing in designing cryptanalysis schemes are also explained in this chapter.

---

[*] Corresponding Author's Email address: siraj.cs@gmail.com.
[†] Corresponding Author's Email: prasadjkc@yahoo.co.in.

Keywords: cryptanalysis, DNA computing, security

1. INTRODUCTION

The concept of Cryptography plays a vital role in ensuring secure communication in various domains. Due to the popularity of machine learning and deep learning techniques, many researchers are developing security frameworks in various domains by incorporating these advanced techniques to ensure secure and reliable communication. Cryptanalysis is also having equal importance as cryptographic schemes because cryptanalysis is required to test and determine the weaknesses of existing cryptographic schemes. The fundamental concept behind the cryptanalysis is to determine the decryption process without knowing the cryptographic algorithm and key employed for encryption.

2. METHODS

2.1. Cryptanalysis of Block Ciphers

The design of Block ciphers is a well-established research area since its inception. The design of block ciphers with adequate security levels against differential and linear cryptanalysis is always been a challenging task [10].

This section explains the advances made in the cryptanalysis of block ciphers. First, we explain Linear, differential and integral cryptanalysis schemes.

Differential analysis is the most prominent attack on block ciphers. This concept brought into light by Biham and Shamir around 1990. The main objective of the differential analysis is to determine the key based on the differences between input and output patterns. Variations in the mapping of plaintext to ciphertext are used to determine the key. In concise, a fixed differential of any plaintext is chosen first and then output the differential of the ciphertext, assigning them with different keys according to different probabilities. By analyzing the ciphertext, the legitimate key can be determined.

Provable security against differential cryptanalysis can be accomplished by finding differential probabilities upper bounded by small enough value [10].

Linear Cryptanalysis comes under known plain text attack. It uses the concept of linear approximation expression between plaintext, ciphertext and the key. Linear approximation can be determined as *ciphertext = f(plaintext,key)* where an attempt is made to find a linear approximation of f. It uses a chain of XOR operations between plaintext and ciphertext bits which are assumed as a linear relationship between plaintext, ciphertext and key bits. It is represented as

$$P[X_1+X_2+\ldots+X_N] \oplus C[Y_1+Y_2+\ldots+Y_M] = K[K_1+K_2+\ldots+K_R]$$

where $X_1, X_2, \ldots X_N$ are plaintext bits and $Y_1, Y_2, \ldots, Y_M$ are the ciphertext bits.

Multiple approximation cryptanalysis is an advancement of linear cryptanalysis because it reduces plaintext pairs that are needed by the ciphertext.

We refer hybrid cryptanalysis as the combination of linear and differential cryptanalysis. The fundamental idea is:

a. To determine some linear approximation.
b. Produce the output differential features pair according to linear approximation making the probability of linear expression correlated with existing linear expression equal to 1.

c. Combining the linear approximation with differential properties leads to the restoration of some key bits.

Integral Cryptanalysis

It is applied to block ciphers that employs bijection component. The fundamental principle of this attack is to restore the key bits by analyzing the values obtained during several rounds of the key transformation [10].

2.2. Cryptanalysis of RSA

RSA is a very popular cryptosystem in use since 1978. It is an asymmetric algorithm whose security levels rely on factoring large numbers. Due to this reason, the cryptanalysis of RSA takes more time or even months and years. This cryptanalysis can be accomplished in a sophisticated amount of time by using an advanced distributed environment or by using some machine learning schemes. Vikrant et al., [9] cryptanalyzed RSA algorithm for any length of key by sharing the workload of cryptanalysis in a distributed environment. They proved that the use of sufficient number of resources will reduce the cryptanalysis time. In their work, they used Quadratic Sieve Factorization Algorithm over a distributed network to reduce the time of cryptanalysis. In this work, they used aglets which are java mobile agents responsible for finding the factors of given n value in a distributed way. These aglets are allowed to communicate with one another by passing messages. In this propounded framework Quadratic Sieve Algorithm (QSA) is executed in a distributed way with the practical implementations of aglets. The process of cryptanalysis is shown in the figure below [9].

It is impractical to use a single system for the cryptanalysis of RSA. Usage of mobile agents for sharing of factorization tasks in a distributed environment will reduce the processing time required for cryptanalysis. This system can cryptanalyze the RSA with any size of keys. Increasing the number of systems reduces the time of cryptanalysis task.

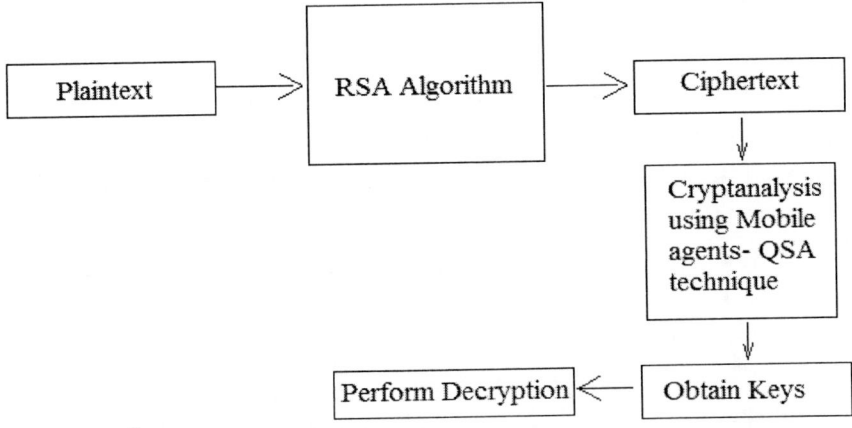

Figure 1. Cryptanalysis of RSA using QSA.

The cryptanalysis results were shown in the following table.

Table 1. Cryptanalysis performance [9]

Value of N	p	q	Number of Systems	Time in Seconds
16843009	257	65537	1	0
			2	0
8030434459	8581	935839	1	10
			2	7
			3	5
123712084919	325309	380291	1	115
			2	74
			3	50

Usage of cloud environment along with machine learning schemes will automate the cryptanalysis tasks within a short span of time. These advanced schemes can be used to make the cryptosystem more powerful than the existing ones.

2.3. Neural Cryptanalysis

Today neural network concepts became prominent in most of the applications. They are not only used for data analysis tasks but also employed in the process of cryptanalysis. Artificial neural networks can be used to automate the task of cryptanalysis. This helps the cryptanalyst to determine the weakness of the cryptosystem being used.

Riccardo Focardi et al. proposed a threat model to determine the weaknesses of classical ciphers [6]. They accomplished the cryptanalysis of these ciphers by introspecting the statistical structure of ciphertext. The neural network was trained by providing statistical features along with the key. With the help of this data, the neural network can predict the key from the given ciphertext. This propounded model automated the cryptanalysis of modern ciphers.

i. Cryptanalysis of Ceaser Ciphers:

This section explains how neural networks can be trained to restore the key by supplying relative frequencies of ciphertext letters to the model. In this model, the frequencies of the characters of ciphertext are measured and frequency histogram was obtained. This obtained histogram was the circular shift of the plain text histogram. From this, it was analyzed that the brute force approach is not required instead a neural network can be trained to determine the relative shift for the frequency histogram. The approach followed is represented by the following steps [6].

    a. Consideration of large dataset of English plaintexts encrypted using random keys

b. Computation of frequencies of each letter in the ciphertext.
c. Training of neural network by giving the frequencies as input and corresponding keys as output.
d. Testing of the network on various independent datasets.

ii. Neural Cryptanalysis of substitution cipher:

Substitution cipher involves the substitution of each letter in plaintext with another. Typically the key is considered as permutation of characters. In this n-grams statistics are maintained. This property is important from an attacker's point of view and it gives the foundation for an attack.

A neural network can be employed to verify the weakness of substitution cipher. Riccardo Focardi et al. used a neural network based on n-grams to introspect how far a given text is from an English one, such that it gives a possibility of applying better substitution, e.g., swapping of two characters [6]. Also, n-grams are required to define a score function that specifies the quality of a given key i.e., how good a given key is and also permits searching for a better one through random swaps. The following steps were used in this model.

a. Considered a big data set of English plaintexts encrypted using random keys.
b. Determine the frequencies of n-grams of both plaintext and ciphertext.
c. Train the neural network by providing the frequencies as input and one bit of output: 1 when the input is plaintext and 0 when the input is ciphertext.
d. Test the neural network on independent datasets.

They also considered an attack strategy that picks a random key, decrypts the ciphertext and uses the neural network to estimate how close the obtained plaintext is to English and, consequently, to the target plaintext. This strategy swaps random letters searching for a suitable plaintext. If the neural network produces a better score then the new key is considered, otherwise again random swap is performed. Goodness value is used to determine how better the new key is. In this way, a neural network can automate part of the cryptanalytic attack.

2.4. AI Based Cryptanalysis

Today, Artificial Intelligence (AI) is the predominant technology used everywhere for automation and analysis tasks irrespective of domains. In this section, some cryptanalysis schemes based on AI techniques are reviewed. Research has been carried out in automating the task of cryptanalysis by using machine learning algorithms. Usage of machine learning algorithms not only determines the weakness of cryptosystem but also assists in the development of strong cryptosystems to ensure a high level of security.

Shaligram Prajapat et al., illustrated the concept of cryptic mining by employing AI techniques [1] [3]. They explained AI enabled cryptosystem that accepts ciphertext and produces the corresponding plaintext. This scheme is recommended in a situation where cryptanalysis intends to obtain plaintext from the ciphertext. AI enabled cryptanalysis scheme proposed by Shaligram Prajapat et al. used on substitution cipher [1], [3]. The problem of generating plaintext from ciphertext comes under the category of intractable problems. In the recommended system a knowledge base is used which comprises of grammar related rules, spellings, vowels, consonants, etc., and also the rules for generating possible combinations of meaningful plaintext from the given ciphertext. This knowledge base is used to perform substitutions in iterations n-grams wise starting with n-gram=1. A pattern matching concept is also employed to generate suitable three word letters. The process of recommended cryptanalysis is shown in Figure 2 below.

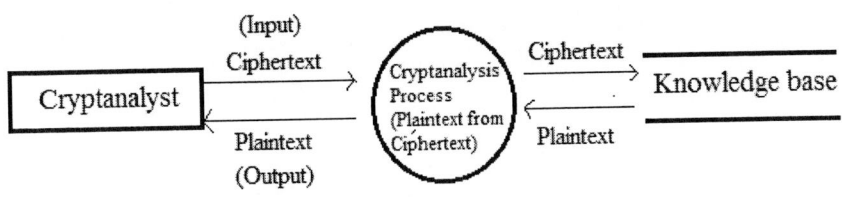

Figure 2. Process of Cryptanalysis.

In Figure 2, cryptanalyst gives ciphertext as input to the cryptanalysis process which in turn gives ciphertext to the knowledge base and then various procedures are executed with respect to the given ciphertext to obtain the meaningful plaintext. The obtained plaintext is the output of the recommended cryptanalysis scheme [1, 3].

Limitations:

a. Works only for substitution and transposition ciphers.
b. Considers only English language based cryptanalysis.
c. It doesn't consider special characters during cryptanalysis.
d. Supports only n-gram $<= 3$.

To perform better cryptanalysis this machine learning algorithms must be used.

Jayachandiran proposed a novel model based on neural networks to perform cryptanalysis on a lightweight cipher called Simon cipher [8]. In this technique, a neural network takes plaintexts along with corresponding ciphertexts to produce the key used for encryption. To accomplish this task neural network is trained to predict the key of plaintext-ciphertext pair. This prediction is made approximation function computed by neurons. This recommended model works well with one round of the Simon cipher [8].

ML algorithms can be used in cryptanalysis to extract the keys from the ciphertext. Similarly, ML algorithms can be merged with the existing cryptanalysis techniques for improving the efficiency in finding the weakness of cryptosystems.

2.5. DNA Based Cryptanalysis

It is one of the most prominent concepts in the field of information and network security. It is an interdisciplinary field that demands DNA based parallel computing infrastructure. As today most of the modern cryptosystems are broken by the use of advanced concepts, the DNA based cryptosystem opens up a new door for ensuring information security [4, 5]. DNA based cryptosystem involves complex bimolecular computations. These biomolecular computations require biological methods that could be implemented through parallel computation. By using this scheme strong cryptosystems can be developed. According to Sattar B et al., biological computations can be performed to produce variants of DNA models [4]. These DNA models could address various NP class of problems. Due to the parallelism nature of DNA models, DNA based cryptanalysis can analyze the cryptosystem in less amount of time. Sattar B et al., also outlined the challenges in this domain which are listed as follows:

a. Transformation of principles of biological concepts from the biological environment to the digital environment.
b. Supports limited ciphers and not tested for other available ciphers.
c. Minimizing the cost of implementation of DNA based computation.
d. It difficult to convert DNA functionality from the bio-environment to the digital-environment.
e. Representation of available data.

As the power of computation is increasing day to day, even advanced cryptographic schemes can be easily broken by the cryptanalyst. In fact, there is a huge demand for innovative and strong algorithms for ensuring information security. To determine the strength and weakness of complex cryptosystem within less time the DNA based cryptanalysis is required. This concept of DNA cryptanalysis lacks the strong and acceptable theory and practical contributions which are nevertheless still a challenging problem to design efficient DNA cryptanalysis schemes.

As DNA computing has many advantages (like parallelism, requires minimum storage, minimum power and long storage time) it can serve the field of cryptanalysis. More research has to be carried out in DNA based cryptography and cryptanalysis [4, 5].

3. FUTURE CHALLENGES

This section flashes the light on the advanced techniques that can be used in cryptanalysis.

- Quantum computing is still in the early phase of research. Applying quantum computing in cryptanalysis of quantum/ post quantum cryptosystems is a challenging task [7].
- ML techniques can be used to determine the keys from the ciphertext. Still, more work has to be done in this area.
- As mentioned earlier, DNA-based computing in cryptanalysis requires more study and gives a new direction of research in cryptanalysis.
- Novel Optimization algorithms can also be used for cryptanalysis. Mohamed Abdel Basset et al. proposed a Novel Whale Optimization Algorithm for cryptanalysis in the Merkle-Hellman cryptosystem.

CONCLUSION

In this chapter, the importance of cryptanalysis was explained along with some recent cryptanalysis schemes. This chapter also outlined the future direction of research in the domain of cryptanalysis and how advanced and emerging techniques can be used for analyzing the complex cryptosystems.

REFERENCES

[1] Shaligram Prajapat, Ramajeevan Thakur, "Cryptic Mining for Automatic Variable Key based Cryptosystem," *Elsevier-Procedia Computer Science* 78 (2016), PP. 199-209.

[2] Mohammad M. Alani, "*Applications of Machine Learning in Cryptography: A Survey,*" https://doi.org/10.1145/3309074.330 9092.

[3] Shaligram Prajapat, Kajol Maheshwari, Aditi Thakur, Ramajeevan Singh Thakur, "Cryptic Mining in Light of Artificial Intelligence", *IJACSA*, Vol.6, No.8, 2015.

[4] Sattar B. Sadkhan, Bassim S. Yaseen, "DNA-Based Cryptanalysis: Challenges, and Future Trends," *2nd Scientific Conference of Computer Science (SCSS), IEEE*, 2019, PP.24-27.

[5] "DNA and DNA Computing in Security Practices-Is the Future in Our Genes?", *GIAC Paper*, SANS Institute 2000-2002.

[6] Riccardo Focardi, Flaminia L. Luccio, "Neural Cryptanalysis of Classical Ciphers," *CEUR-WS-org*/Vol-2243/paper10.pdf.

[7] Stephen P. Jordan, Yi-Kai Liu, "Quantum Cryptanalysis: Shor, Grover, and Beyond," *IEEE Computer and Reliable Societies*, Sep-Oct 2018.

[8] Kowsic Jayachandiran, "A Machine Learning Approach for Cryptanalysis", *RIT Compute Science, Capstone Report 20175*.

[9] Vikrant Shende, Giridhar Sudi, Meghana Kulkarni, "*Fast Cryptanalysis of RSA Encrypted Data Using A combination of Mathematical and Brute Force Attack in Distributed Computing Environment,*" *ICPCSI*-2017, PP.2446-2449.

[10] Xu Dewu, Chen Wei, "A Survey on Cryptanalysis of Block Ciphers", *ICCASM*-2010, V-8, PP. 218-220.

[11] Harshali D. Zodpe, Prakash W. Wani, "Design and Implementation of Algorithm for DES Cryptanalysis," 12th *International Conference on Hybrid Intelligence System (HIS) IEEE*-2012.

Chapter 4

ROLE OF PENETRATION TESTING IN SECURITY ANALYSIS

Ch. Rupa[*]

Department of CSE, VR Siddhartha Engineering College,
Vijayawada, Andhra Pradesh

ABSTRACT

An important phase of system design development is security analysis. Vulnerability assessment and cryptanalysis are part of security analysis. Various tools, techniques, and approaches have been used while doing security analysis. These can apply by considering certain permits like the strength of security key, ciphertext, encryption algorithms, storage protection, implementation languages and like some other factors. As a part of this Penetration (PEN) test has to be used by the analyzers to know the strength of their approach or method or methodology used for implementing the system. In this chapter detailed description presented on Penetration testing phases and its functioning. The main strength of this paper is a list of various tools under each phase with the description has mentioned.

---

[*] Corresponding Author's Email: rupamtech@gmail.com.

Keywords: Sensitive data, Vulnerability Assessment, Nessus Tool, Nmap

INTRODUCTION

A penetration test also called a pen test. It has used to evaluate system security. So the pen test also referred to as an authorized simulator attack on a system. It can help to set a fine web application firewall (WAF) policies and patches for detected vulnerabilities. In the 1970's, the Department of Defense used this method for demonstrating the vulnerabilities in the system. The main objective of the pen test is to identify security vulnerabilities in the network infrastructure of an organization. Security is not a single point solution but is a process of requirement. Pentest can be done by using various methods such as

a. External Test :

Its target visible assets of a company on the Internet (Ex. Website, DNS, E-mail, etc) and it has tested from an external entity (from outside the organizational network). Either Internet or Extranet (a private network) has used to perform this test.

b. Internal Test:

It's target to access an application behind the firewall simulation attack by the insider maybe greedy employee, etc and this process done by the internal entity only.

c. Blind Test:

It aims to simulate the real hacker actions and procedures at organization premises by prior limited notification to the concerned people at an organization. The testing team uses publicly available sources (like USENET, Domain Name Registry, other Internet

Discussion boards, etc) to gather the organization information for doing simulation.

d. Double Blind Test:
It is an extension of the blind test. Test the system as an attacker without provided prior to additional information. In this, monitors escalation and response procedures, incident identification, etc.

e. Targeted Test:
It involves both the organizational team and the pen test team together. This is a valuable and cost-effective exercise.

PEN TEST PHASES

Pentest phases which can be done by authorized attackers, for reducing exploitation of the vulnerabilities in the system by unauthorized attackers through preliminary patches are as shown in Figure 1.

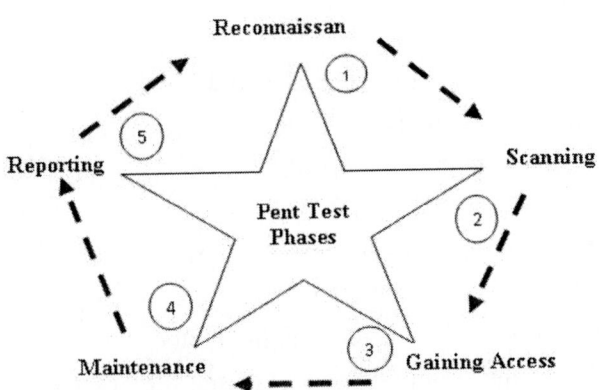

Figure 1. Penetration Testing Phases.

The penetration testing process divided into five stages such as Reconnaissance, Scanning, Gaining Access, Maintenance and Reporting.

Reconnaissance – Define the Scope and goals of a test and gathers the intelligence in this phase.

Scanning – Analyze various target applications how can they respond for the Intruder attempts.

Gaining Access / Exploitation – Try to exploit the uncover vulnerabilities for understanding the damage rate by the attackers.

Maintaining Access – Try to gather more information from the target environment by taking persistent steps.

Reporting – Compiled the test results into a report for organization reference purposes which can help to configure their policies and other applications.

METHODS

Reconnaissance

Footprinting is a part of reconnaissance which can be the blueprint of the organization's security profile. At this phase, the only tester can set up the scope and objectives of the test. Gather the target information as much as possible either from internal or external sources. Inside sources of the target (ex: organization) which can cause to help to collect information are Internal DNS, Dumpster Diving, Shoulder Surfing, Private Websites, Eves Dropping, etc.

As same as the External sources of the target that can be used for gathering the information are phone, Email-Headers, Websites, Search Engines (Ex: Google), WHOIS, Social Networks, Customers, IPR (Intellectual Property Rights), etc. This gathered information

(Intelligence) used to a better understanding of how a target attacked by unauthorized persons and analyzed the possible ways to exploit the identified vulnerabilities. At the end of this phase, the tester expected to have IP address lists of a target that can scan later as shown in Figure 2.

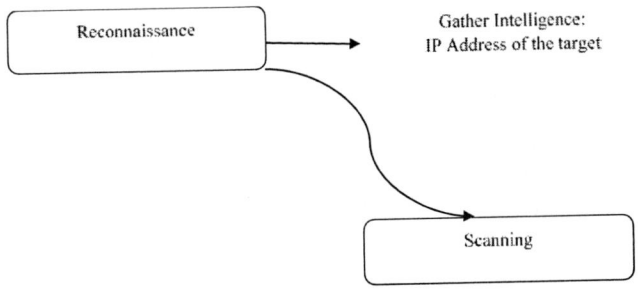

Figure 2. Reconnaissance State Chart

Table 1 shows that various sample activity tools for doing Reconnaissance or Footprinting on a specified target for intelligence gathering.

Table 1. Reconnaissance Activity Tools

S. No	Free Tools	Description
1.	AnyWho	To find the information on People
2.	Nslookup	To obtain an IP Address or any specific DNS record.
3.	Path Analyzer Pro	To investigate network issues with network trace routing deliverables.
4.	Ping	To test source ability to reach a specific destination
5.	Tracert	To display the routes and measuring transit delays of the packets.
6.	Spokeo.com	People search Website which can aggregate information from online and offline
7.	Netcraft	To gather information about the web servers
8.	Social Engineering	Ex: Facebook, WhatsApp, Linkedin, etc
9.	The harvester	It is like a catalog with a list of email addresses and subdomains
10.	Search Engines	Ex: Google, Bing, etc.

Scanning

A pen tester tries to gain access to the target system as well as tries to gain much information about the target in order to detect the vulnerabilities in the system. This phase helps to understand how to target application will respond to different attacker attempts. This can be analyzed by using two ways.

Statistical Analysis – Application code analyzed to estimate how it will respond while running.

Dynamic Analysis – Application code analyzed while it was in running state.

This can be reached by two activities of the scanning phase are vulnerability scanning and Port scanning. Vulnerability scanning has used to identify the weakness in the related target servers and software. As well as, port scanning has used to know the status of the ports whether the target ports opened or not. Once you find the list of open ports by port scanning, the later step is for looking at the server vulnerabilities (weakness) by doing vulnerability scanning.

While doing scanning in the process of Pen test, initially, identify the state of the host (target) whether it was alive (up) or not (down). If the host was in the live state then go to ports or services scanning for knowing their status. In OSI networking model, Network Layer as layer 3 has some protocols such as IPv4, IPv6, and ICMP, as well as Transport Layer as layer 4 has some protocols, are TCP (SRAF UP - Flags) and UDP (doesn't have flags) plays an important role in the pen test scanning. With the reference of flags setup status in TCP, can possible to identify the target IP address and other actions. So it needs to give protection to the flag status by using Encryption ciphers.

Some of the basic techniques used for doing scanning are

- Ping Sweep
- Subnet Mask
- 3-way handshaking and
- Banner Grabbing, etc

Also, advanced scanning techniques used for emphasizing the performance of scanning results. In order to this tester can able to use the following techniques

- Anonymizers
- Proxies
- Fragmentation
- Spoofing

At the end of the phase, the tester can able to understand the weaknesses in the system by knowing the list of open ports and running servers information which can be required to exploit further as shown in Figure 3.

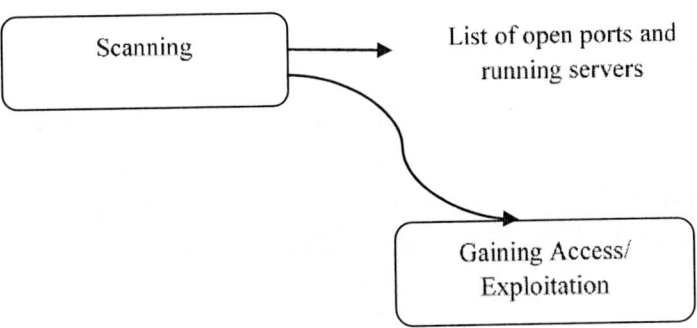

Figure 3. Reconnaissance State Chart.

Table 2 shows that various sample activity tools for doing Scanning for doing port scanning and vulnerability scanning.

Table 2. Scanning Activity Tools

S. No	Activity	Tools	Description
1.	Port Scanning	Nmap	To find whether the ports are open or close
2.	Port Scanning	Zenmap	Graphical Interface tool to know the status of the port
3.	Vulnerability scanning	Nessus	To investigate the weaknesses in the servers
4.	Vulnerability scanning	Nexpose	Vulnerability Scanner
5.	Web Server Scanner	Nikto	It is an open-source tool that provides test reports of websites. It performs around 6000 tests against a website.
6.	Web Application Scanner	OWASP	It refers to the Open Web Application Security Project. It is an organization that gives a scanning report to the computer and internet- based applications.
7.	Port Scanning	Hping, Fin Scan, Null Scan, Xmas Scan	TCP/IP packet analyzer

Gaining Access

Testers will try to exploit the identified vulnerabilities through the scanning stage report. In order to this, they may be dependent on the number of web application attacks such as SQL injection attack, XSS (Cross-site scripting) attacks, Buffer Overflow attack, Session Hijacking, etc. These can give support to the tester (as an attacker) for stealing the data and to interrupt the network and DOS attacks (Denial of Service) etc. For example, in 2016, Dyn Cyber Attack that caused major internet services unavailable to the intermediate devices. It was a distributed denial service (DDOS) attack. The next major attack was, in 2017, WannaCry Ransomware Attack which targeted the Microsoft Windows Operating system based computers. It was encrypted the data and demanded the payments in cryptocurrency for releasing the key to do the decryption.

To overcome these kinds of attacks, pen testers can do real attempts on identified disclosed weaknesses to access the information. It may cause to develop the immediate patches to respective vulnerabilities.

As shown in Figure 4, in this phase tester can able to understand the how and where patches are required on identified vulnerabilities by scanning resources. In order to this pen tester should know exploitation of the system causes also.

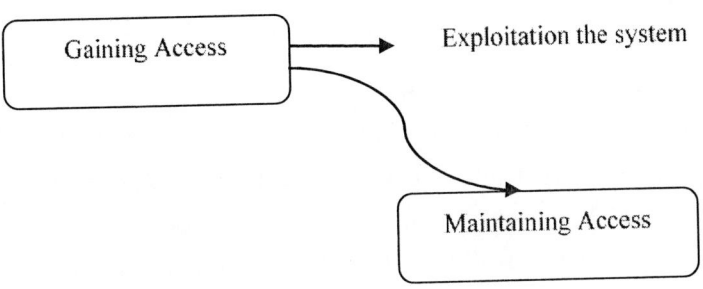

Figure 4. Gaining Access State Chart.

Table 3 gives a list of tools that have used by the Pen testers for trying to exploit the system through identified vulnerabilities.

Table 3. Gaining Access Tools

S. No	Tools	Description
1.	Metaspoilt	To find whether the ports are open or close
2.	Zenmap	Graphical Interface tool to know the status of the port
3.	Nessus	To investigate the weaknesses in the servers
4.	Nexpose	Vulnerability Scanner
5.	Hping	TCP/IP packet analyzer
6.	Fin Scan Null Scan Xmas Scan	TCP/IP packet Scanner

Maintaining Access

The main aim of this phase connected with the target system by establishing access through persistence connections. These connections can use to attack the machine successfully and have full command on the victim machine. Generally, organizational networks and ports connections have protected by the firewall. This task can become easy by the firewall or any one of the systems from the networking has compromised through persistent connections.

It extends to that pen tester may use sniffer for intercepting inbound network traffic, outbound network traffic, FTP (File Transfer Protocol) and telnet sessions. Later he could transmit the data as per his requirement. To get success in this phase, either attackers or testers can choose Trojan horses, Rootkits, Backdoors and covert channels, etc as shown in Figure 5 to exhilarate the required data. Recently, in July 2018, Advanced Persistent threats against institutions are big bang in the Middle East, specifically at Palestinian. Attackers used phishing emails as a Trojan horse for distracting the targets.

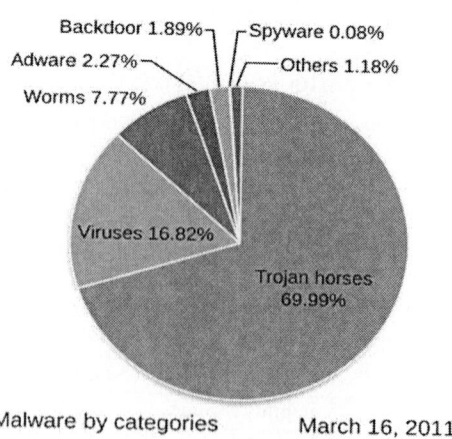

(Source: Wikipedia by Kizar)

Figure 5. Different Tools and methods for maintain access.

Role of Penetration Testing in Security Analysis

At this phase, APT (Advanced Persistent threats) attacks also verified by the pen testers by imitated them and look at if a vulnerability can be used to maintain access or not. APT attacks are differing from traditional attacks. These are significantly complex. In order to do these attacks, the attacker chooses the target very carefully by research. Its consequences also are vast. Ex: Compromising employee's data from a large enterprise.

Figure 6 shows that the objectives of Maintain Access of the pen tester. Initially, establish the required infrastructure for accessing the data from the identified vulnerabilities. Later extract the data. Next, that result has transformed for generating the report.

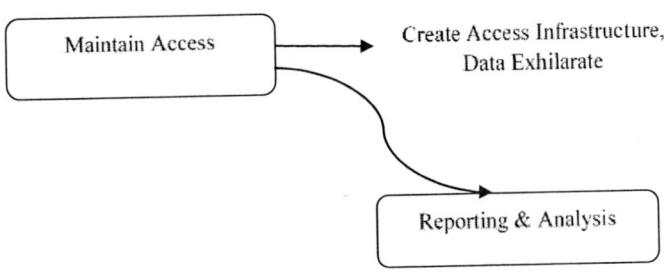

Figure 6. Maintain Access State Chart.

Table 4. Gaining Access Tools

S. No	Activity	Tools	Description
1.	Trojan horse	• Metaspoilt • King Phisher	Compromise the system from fake information which looks like legitimate (ex: Website)

2.	Backdoors	• Software Key Logger
		  1. Revealer
		  2. REFOG
		• Hardware Key Logger
			Action of recording the keystrokes.

3.	Covert Channel	Nmap SRM tools Gypsy Flow Analyzer	Vulnerability Scanner
4.	Rootkit analyzer	Antivirus software like Kaspersky, McAfee, Avast, etc.	Scanning of Signatures and analysis of memory dumps

Maintain Access can perform by using various tools. Sample list of tools shown in Table 4. Mostly used tool for access gaining from the target system is Metaspoilt. Most of the attackers preferred to do phishing attacks by these kinds of tools.

Reporting and Analysis

The penetration test results should compile into a report. It consists of detailed information on specific vulnerabilities that were exploited and accessed the data nothing but refereed to as sensitive data. But time is taken by the system to detect the pen tester. This report is useful to reduce the attacks on an application and to configure and upgrade the WAF (Web Application Firewalls). This task is mandatory before going to test any application again.

Finally, a pen test should be satisfied with certain compliance requirements for security auditing purpose that includes PCI DSS (Payment Card Industry Data Security Standard) and SOC, etc. Some of these standards were satisfied only by using certified WAF because these can run based on five security service principles Such as

- Privacy
- Security
- Availability
- Confidentiality
- Integrity

It is a cycling process as shown in Figure 7. After configuring the WAF based on the analysis report given by the pen tester, again process will start with Reconnaissance. Reporting is a key deliverable in the pen testing process.

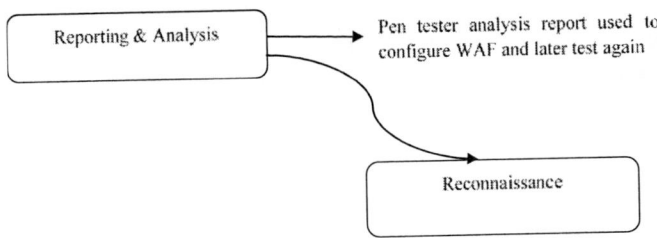

Figure 7. Maintain Access State Chart.

Pentest reporting tools listed in Table 5. These tools are very useful to store the results up to date for quick reference. Khali Linux is useful to run easily the following tools.

Table 5. Reporting Tools

S. No	Tools	Description
1.	Dradis	<ul><li>Web Application.</li><li>It provides a central repository.</li><li>It helps to keep track, to generate reports easily</li></ul>
2.	Magic Tree	<ul><li>It is a Kali Tool.</li><li>It helps for data consolidation, Querying and report generation.</li></ul>
3.	Metagoofil	It uses to extract public document metadata

Results and Vulnerability Analysis

Nessus tool uses to evaluate vulnerability assessment based on certain attributes. The following steps show the functioning of the tool.

- Nessus is a network vulnerability scanner developed by Tenable Network Security. It is free of charge for personal use in a non-enterprise environment.
- It searches map systems for weakness in the application, computer or their network. It identifies both the internal and external network scans.

- Internal scan means scanning is performed within a particular router. External scan means scanning involves the hosts outside the particular router or a remote host. Nessus has the capability of multiple scanning of the hosts at the same time.
- The main advantage is that Nessus makes no assumptions for what services are running on what ports and it actively attempts to exploit identifies vulnerabilities.
- Nessus is based on a client-server architecture. Each session is controlled by the client and the test is run on the server-side.
- Nessus allows scans for the following types of vulnerabilities:
- Vulnerabilities that allow a remote hacker to control or access sensitive data on a system.
- Misconfiguration (e.g., open mail relay, missing patches, etc.).
- Default passwords, a few common passwords, and blank/absent passwords on some system accounts. Nessus can also call Hydra (an external tool) to launch a dictionary attack.
- Denials of service against the TCP/IP stack by using malformed packets.
- Preparation for PCI DSS audits.

CONCLUSION

Testing an application system, network or computer system required to check the status of security vulnerabilities. This report helps to resolve identified issues that can require protecting the system from unauthorized activities by the intruders. A practice of testing should need to perform by the designers and developers through Penetration testing to know the security status of the system. It refers to a security analysis that can perform either manually or automatically with some software applications. This chapter has discussed role of penetration testing in security analysis as well as listed various software applications to perform it.

In: A Closer Look at Cybersecurity ...
Editors: Ch. Rupa et al.
ISBN: 978-1-53618-165-4
© 2020 Nova Science Publishers, Inc.

Chapter 5

VULNERABILITY ASSESSMENT USING NESSUS TOOL

Ch. Rupa
Department of C.S.E, V.R Siddhartha Engineering College,
Vijayawada, Andhra Pradesh, India

ABSTRACT

There are number of techniques and tools available to list the vulnerabilities present in the remote host. Vulnerability assessment plays an important role in securing the organizations network system. The Nessus vulnerability scanner is the world-leader in active scanners, featuring high-speed discovery, configuration auditing, and asset profiling, sensitive data discovery and vulnerability analysis of our security posture. Nessus have the capability to discover the state of port and also it detects the flaws on particular system with a recommended solution to fix it. Nessus can import scan results done by another tools like Nmap etc. and perform vulnerability scan accordingly. It makes the top managements work easier for network security.

Keywords: sensitive data, vulnerability assessment, Nessus tool, Nmap

1. INTRODUCTION

Nessus Tool uses to evaluate vulnerability assement based on certain attributes. The following steps show that functioning of the tool.

- Nessus is a network vulnerability scanner developed by Tenable Network Security. It is free of charge for personal use in a non-enterprise environment.
- It searches map systems for weakness in application, computer or their network. It identifies both internal and external network scan.
- Internal scan means scanning is performed within a particular router. External scan means scanning involves the hosts outside the particular router or a remote host. Nessus has the capability to multiple scanning of the hosts at a same time.
- The main advantage is that Nessus makes no assumptions for what services are running on what ports and it actively attempts to exploit identifies vulnerabilities.
- Nessus is based on client-server architecture. Each session is controlled by the client and the test is run on the server side.

Nessus allows scans for the following types of vulnerabilities:

- Vulnerabilities that allow a remote hacker to control or access sensitive data on a system.
- Misconfiguration (e.g., open mail relay, missing patches, etc.).
- Default passwords, a few common passwords, and blank/absent passwords on some system accounts. Nessus can also call Hydra (an external tool) to launch a dictionary attack.
- Denials of service against the TCP/IP stack by using malformed packets.
- Preparation for PCI DSS audits.

2. INSTALLATION OF NESSUS TOOL

Open the browser and search for Download Nessus. Open the link highlighted below i.e., official website of Nessus www.tenable.comto download the vulnerability scanner. The exact link to download Nessus is https://www.tenable.com/products/nessus/select-your-operating-system as shown in Figure 1.

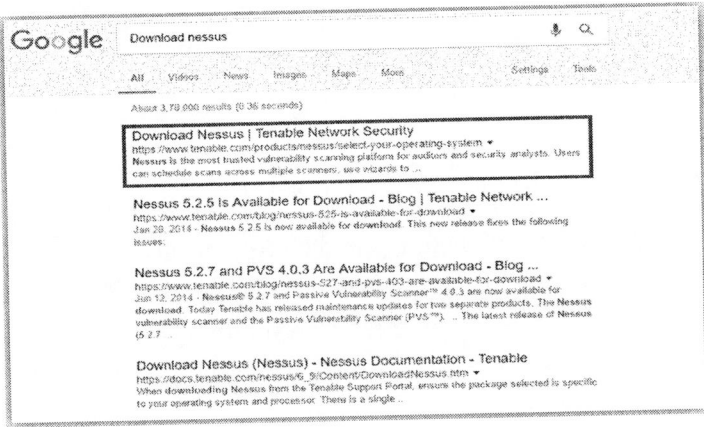

Figure 1. Download link of Nessus Tool.

Download Nessus according to the OS and system requirement from the left side of the page as shown in Figure 2.

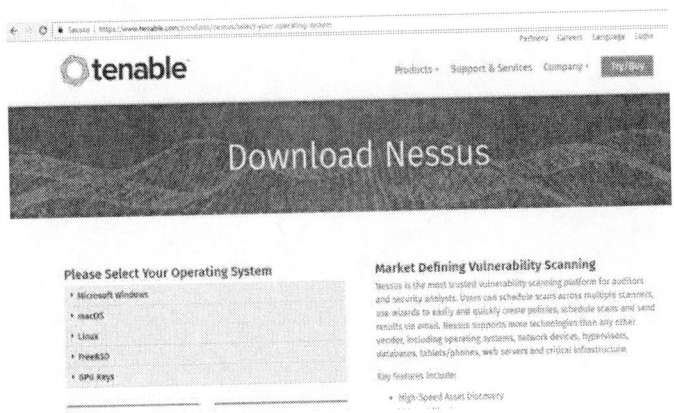

Figure 2. Nessus Download otions based on OS.

Click on the file Nessus-6.10.2-x64 that is downloaded and run the application. Setup and Run options of Nessus looks like shown in as shown in Figure 3.

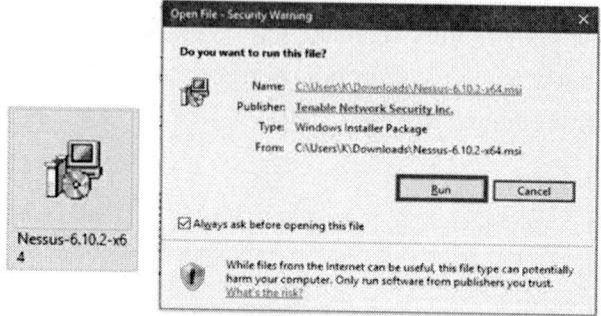

Figure 3. Download and run options of Nessus Tool.

After the installation is complete the browser opens a page showing Welcome to Nessus. Figure 4 shows that the process of installation of Nessus Tool. Click on Click here -> Continue to this webpage -> Continue and set up an initial account which will be an administrator account and click Continue.

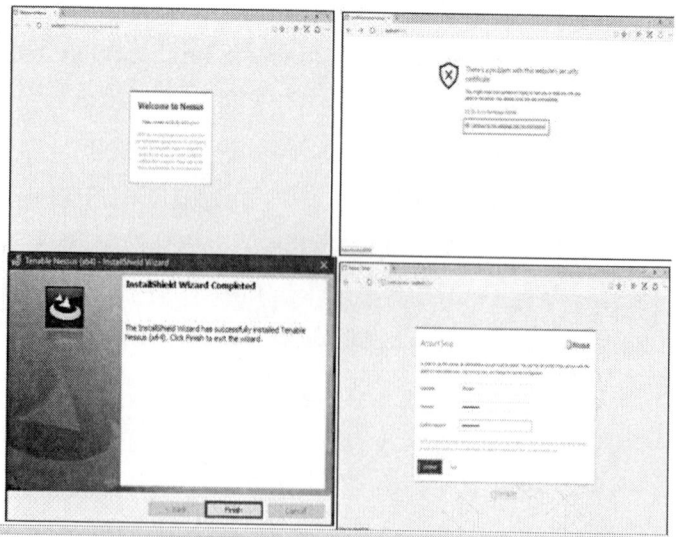

Figure 4. Nessus tool installation process.

Vulnerability Assesment Using Nessus Tool

Then a Registration page opens asking for the activation code. Under the registration select from drop down menu as Nessus(Home, Professional or Manager) and since we don't have an activation code click on Registering this scanner which is highlighted.

A new tab opens for registration purpose where we can mention the type of Nessus account we need. We will continue with the Free Version of Nessus Home. Click on Register Now. In this step, we have to register to get an activation code. Fill the details such as First Name, Last Name, Email, Country, and check the box I agree to the terms of service and click Register. Following Figure 5 and Figure 6 represent the registration process of the tool.

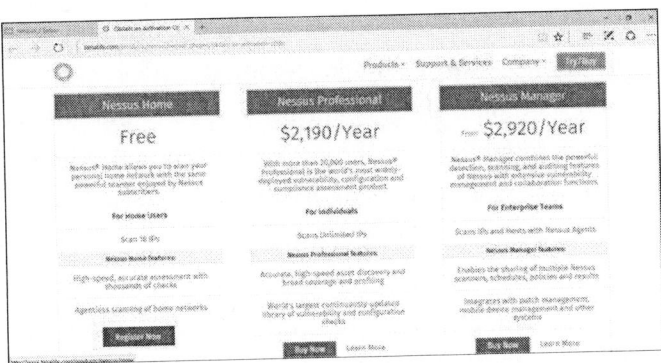

Figure 5. Registeration.

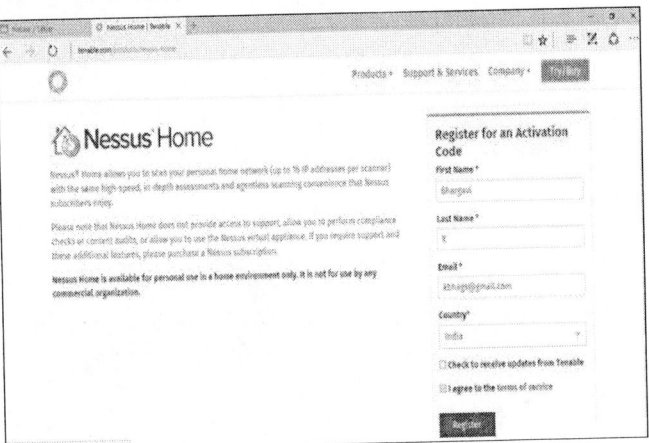

Figure 6. Nessus Home Page.

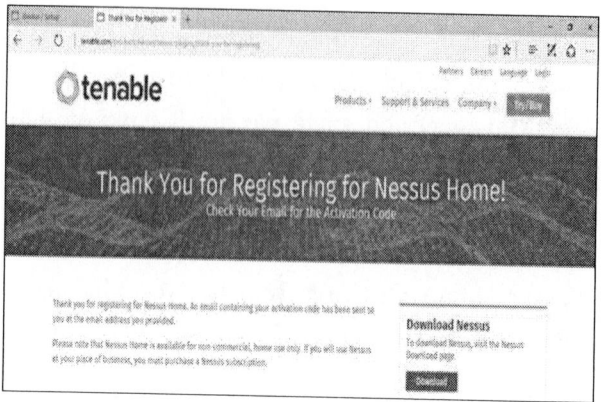

Figure 7. Completion of registration.

Now *open the Email* to check the activation code. Copy the code and paste it in the activation code area asked in the Registration page and click *Continue*. The setup is completed now and Nessus will download and compile the plugins. Once the plugins have been downloaded and compiled, the Nessus UI will initialize and the Nessus server will start. After initialization, Nessus is ready for use.

After initialization, *Login* screen will be displayed and the Nessus product you are connecting to via the Web UI is shown. Using the administrative credentials created during the installation, log in to the Nessus interface to verify the access. Once authenticated, click the gear icon (Settings) to view information about Nessus and the plugin set.

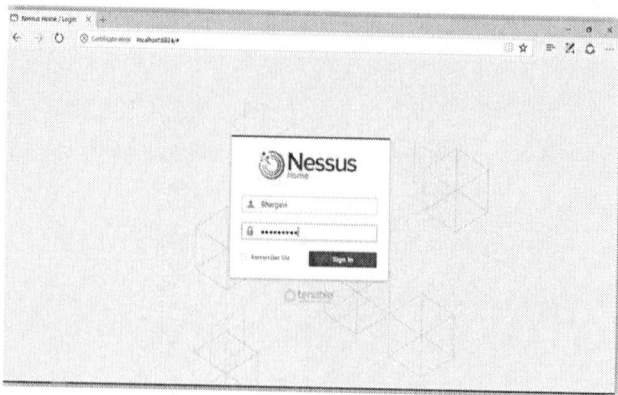

Figure 8. Login screen.

3. FUNCTIONING OF NESSUS TOOL

STEP 1: Nessus runs on local host with port number 8834. Click on *Policies ->New Policy*

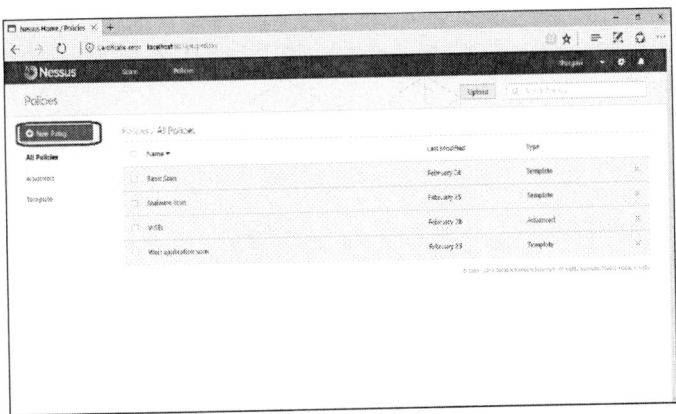

Figure 9. New Policy.

STEP 2: Select *Basic Network Scan* -> Enter the name of the scan -> *Save*

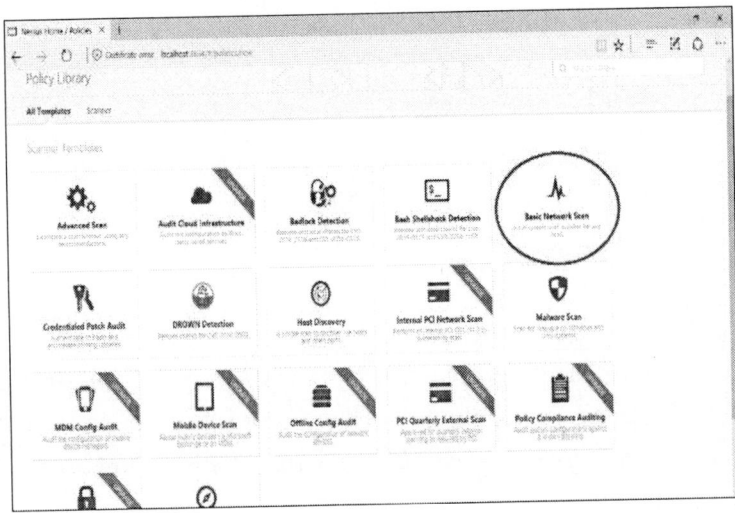

Figure 10. Selection of Basic Network Scan.

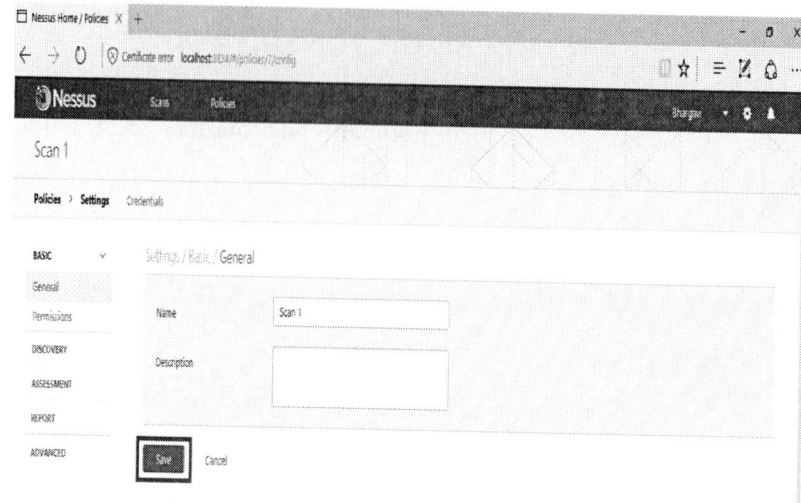

Figure 11. Entering options.

Go to Scan -> *New Scan* -> *Basic Network Scan*

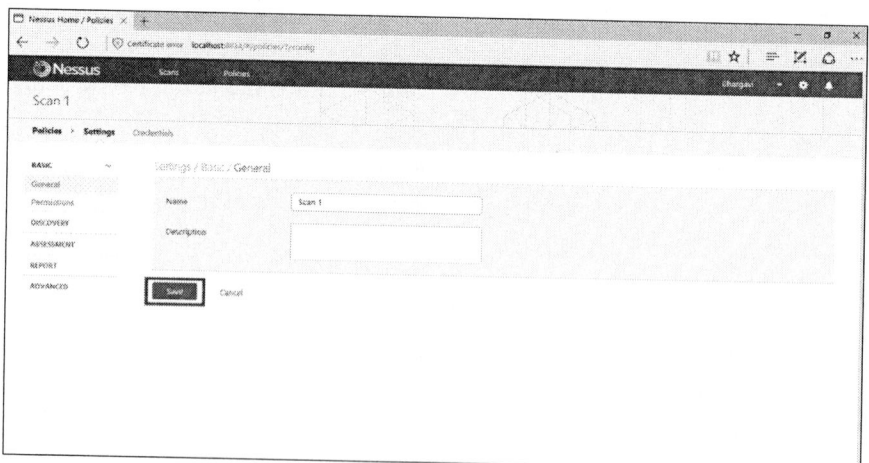

Figure 12. Saving options.

In this step, enter the *IP address* or the *Domain Name* to start the scan and Click the *Save* button. We have saved the scan name as *Scan1* and had given *http://www.vrsiddhartha.ac.in/* asthe domain name and launched the scan.

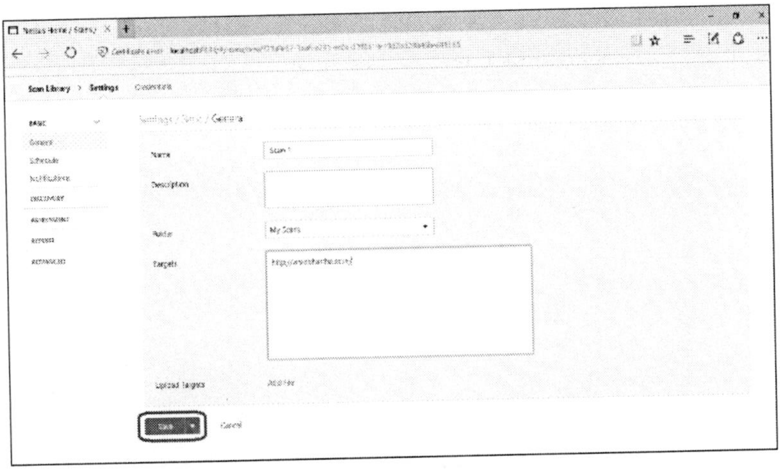

Vulnerability Assesment Using Nessus Tool

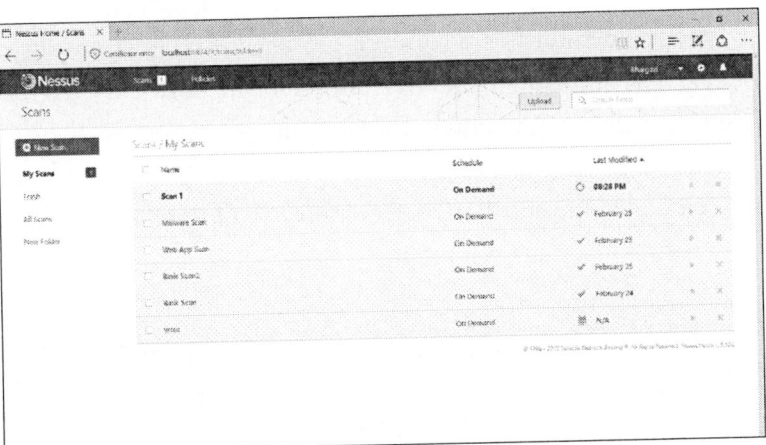

Figure 13. Specifying domain name.

Figure 14. Scan process.

The scan is completed now and it divided all the vulnerabilities present in the host in to 5 types based upon the threat level.

- Critical(Red)-11
- High(Orange)- 14
- Medium(Yellow)-15
- Low(Green)-3
- Info(Blue)-43

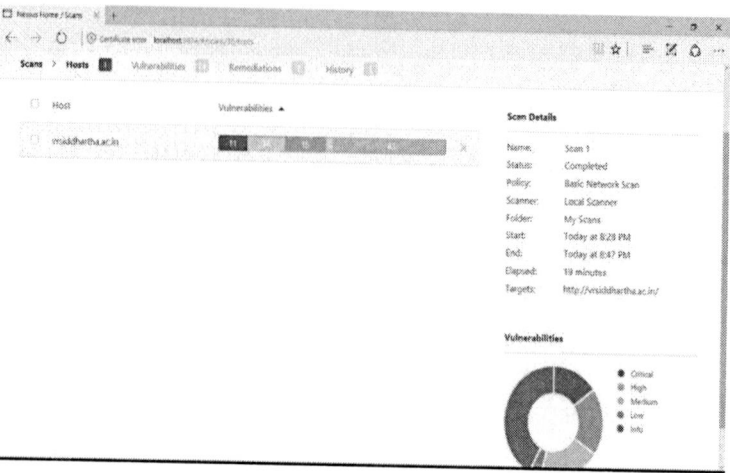

Figure 15. Scan details and vulnerabilites.

All the Vulnerabilities which are present in the host are displayed below. It is also showing us the IP Address of the host and time taken to complete the scan. By clicking on each link we can view the detailed information regarding the vulnerability. From the below pic let us select the first critical condition *PHP 5.5.x < 5.5.14 Multiple Vulnerabilities*.

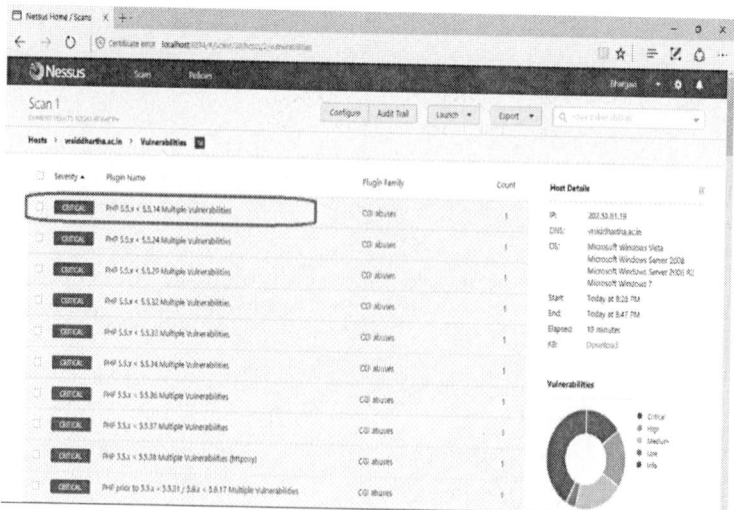

Figure 16. Details of vulnerability.

Vulnerability Assesment Using Nessus Tool 59

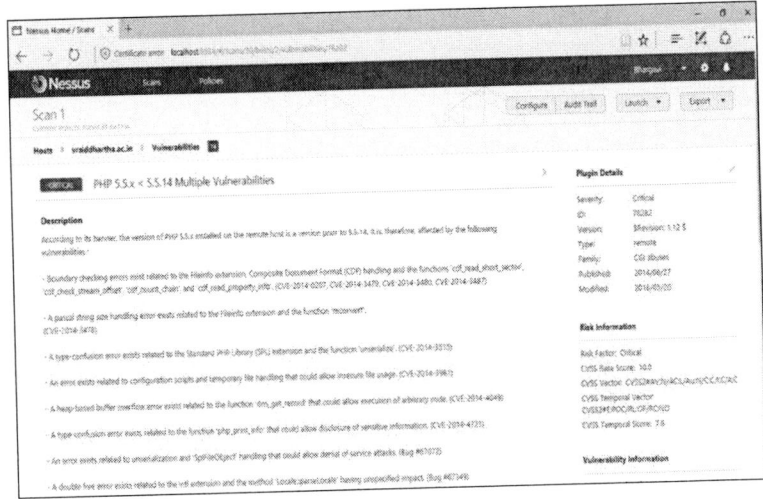

Figure 17. Description of vulnerability.

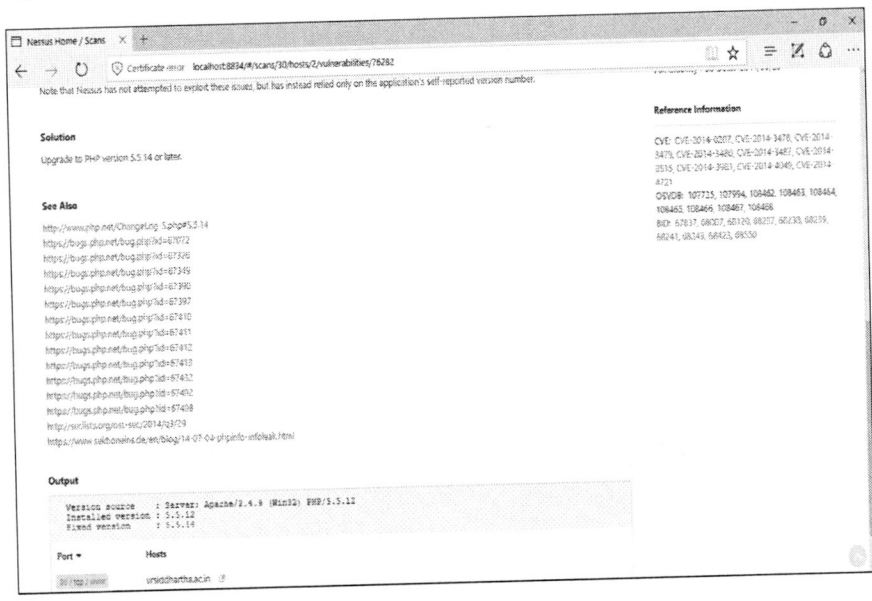

Figure 18. Version details.

After the critical vulnerabilities, let us select one High risk factor vulnerability and see the information. Let us select *Apache 2.4.x < 2.4.10 Multiple Vunerabilities* and see the details.

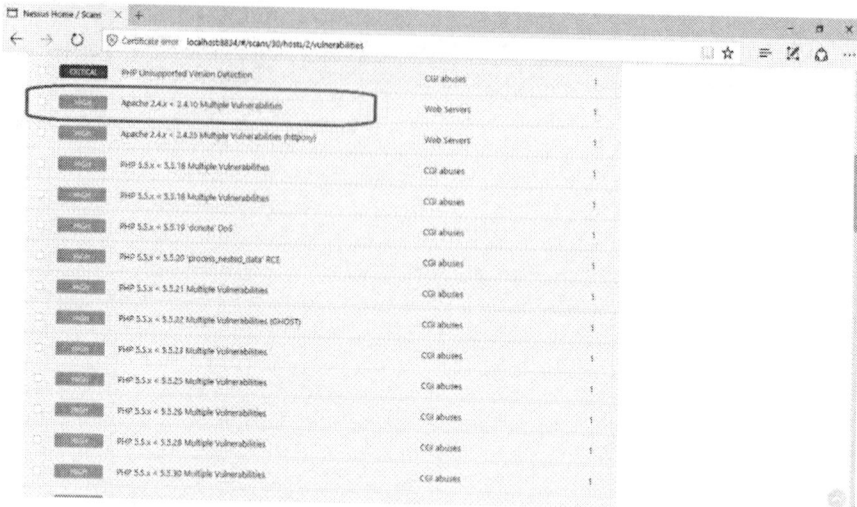

Figure 19. Multiple vunerabilities.

We can view other vulnerabilities from Medium, Low Categories also.

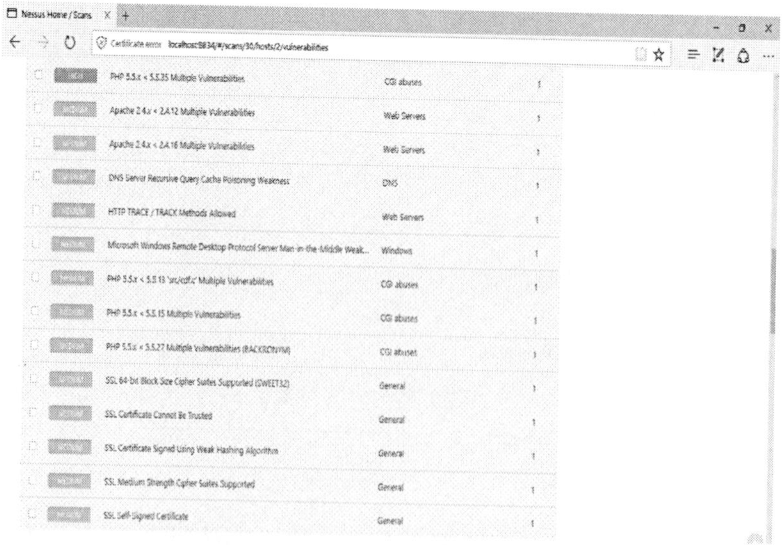

Figure 20. Vulnerabilities categories.

Let us see the Info Vulnerability by clicking on the *Nessus SYN Scanner*.

Vulnerability Assesment Using Nessus Tool 61

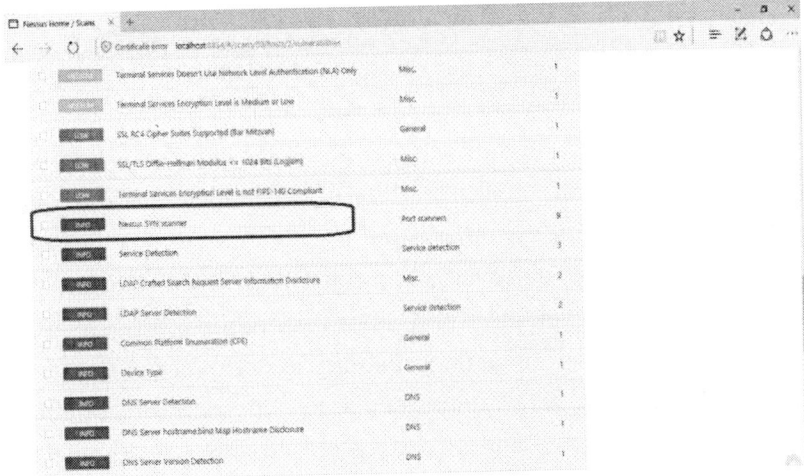

Figure 21. Selecting Nessus SYN scanner.

Not only displaying the vulnerabilities present in the host, Nessus Vulnerability Scanner will also list us the *Remediations* (immediate actions) to be done which will resolve the vulnerabilities on the network as shown in Figure 21.

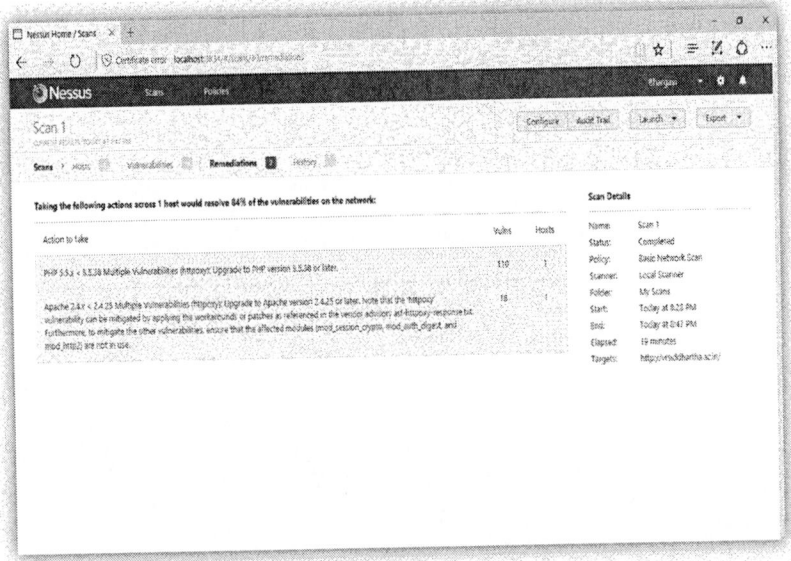

Figure 22. Remediations list.

Conclusion

There are number of techniques and tools available to list the vulnerabilities present in the remote host. Vulnerability assessment plays an important role in securing the organizations network system. The Nessus vulnerability scanner is the world-leader in active scanners, featuring high-speed discovery, configuration auditing, and asset profiling, sensitive data discovery and vulnerability analysis of our security posture. Nessus have the capability to discover the state of port and also it detects the flaws on particular system with a recommended solution to fix it. Nessus can import scan results done by another tools like Nmap etc. and perform vulnerability scan accordingly. It makes the top managements work easier for network security.

In: A Closer Look at Cybersecurity ...
Editors: Ch. Rupa et al.
ISBN: 978-1-53618-165-4
© 2020 Nova Science Publishers, Inc.

Chapter 6

DIGITIZATION WITH CYBER SECURITY AND AI: A REVIEW

S. Gopi Krishna[1,], Mohammd Sirajuddin[2,†] and S. Suresh Babu[1,‡]*

[1]C.S.E, Sri Mittapalli College of Engineerig, Guntur,
Andhra Pradesh, India

[2]C.S.E, Koneru Lakshmaiah Education Foundation (KLEF),
Guntur, Andhra Pradesh, India

ABSTRACT

Due to the rapid advancement in technology, Digitization has become prominent in today's society. To empower society in an efficient and effective way every nation is focusing to achieve digitalization. Digitization is important for storing, accessing and sharing information. Digitization presents new security threats and challenges that should be addressed by cyber security schemes. In this chapter, we explained the

---

[*] Corresponding Author's Email: gks2405@gmail.com.
[†] Corresponding Author's Email: Email:siraj.cs@gmail.com.
[‡] Corresponding Author's Email: cse.sureshbabu@gmail.com.

importance of cyber security in digitization. We also explained the role of AI in developing cyber security schemes to protect the digital world from various attacks.

Keywords: digitization, attacks, AI based cyber security

1. INTRODUCTION

Today's era is known as an era of *machine and technology*. To empower society in an efficient and effective way every nation is focusing to achieve *digitalization*. Smart electronic devices have made our life easy and comfortable. Digitalization is completely dealing with data. In different forms data is shared everywhere. Sometimes data is very sensitive and can be misused by anyone. Indeed companies and organizations should make sure when sharing sensitive information, it is very essential to keep the data safe. Moreover, when the government, military, banking, and other organizations work with data, it must be taken well care by using some security techniques [1]. This is where *Cyber security* plays an important role.

According to NIST (National Institute of Standards and Technology), Cyber Security is the protection of assets from unauthorized activities in order to ensure confidentiality, integrity, and availability. These three concepts are known as CIA.

The main goal of cyber security mechanisms is to support CIA by using the latest technologies.

According to NIST, cyber security framework consists of five components as shown in Figure 1.

The number of cybercrimes [2] are vastly increasing. It can also be termed as *Information Technology Security*. The main reason behind the cybercrimes is extreme usage of technology and the lack of advanced techniques to protect data and the legitimate user. In this case, *cyber security* is the mechanism needed to maintain the data/assets safe. Let us have look at its types, requirements, merits and challenges.

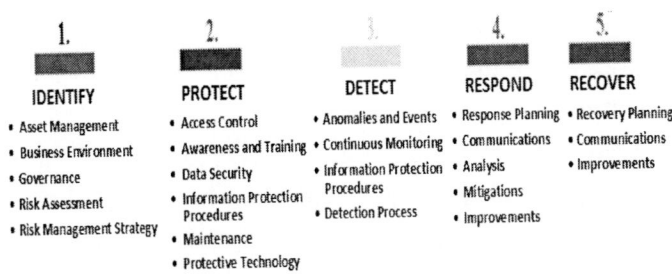

Figure 1. Cyber Security Framework.

1.1. Types of Threats

There are a few threats of Information security as confirmed by [3]

1. *Malware:* It is a harmful and malicious program that stops the functioning of the entire system.
2. *Botnet:* It is a malware. Today botnets became the biggest security threat. A botnet consists of a collection of devices interconnected to launch cybercrime. These interconnected devices are controlled by bootmaster. Criminals use botnets to launch DoS (Denial of Service) attack.
3. *Social Engineering:* It is the change in people's behavior to indulge in wrong actions with data. The types include Phishing, Baiting, Vishing etc.
    - Phishing: In this attack, trusted resource is imitated to get personal information of people. This attack makes the people to access fake emails or websites where they are forced to enter their personal account information. Eg: Attacker sends fake emails from the reputed financial

organization requesting for banking related information (like credit card/debit card).
- Baiting: This attack is launched by relying on the greed/curiosity of the people. In this, attacker gives fake offers to the people to get their personal and sensitive information. This attack encourages people to download malwares by surrendering their personal information.
- Vishing: This attack is launched through VoIP (Voice over IP). It involves spoofing of legitimate phone numbers that lead the people to believe that the call is legitimate and share their information.

4. *Ransomware:* Another class of malware from cryptovirology that terrorizing and manipulating public data or suppressing it without their knowledge.
5. *Backdoors:* It allows access to the assets without the user's knowledge.
6. *Cryptojacking:* As we know that cryptocurrency is a part of digitization where digital currency is used for the exchange of goods and services. Cryptojacking is a malicious cryto-mining software used by unauthorized people to mine cryptocurrency.
7. *Formjacking:* As we know that in today's digital work, all payments are made by customers through online. As all the bank transactions are digitized, it gives a chance for criminals to insert malicious javascript code into payment application to seize the customer details. This type of attacks are increasing day by day across the globe.

1.2. Major Domains

The following are the areas of computer security as shown in Figure 2.

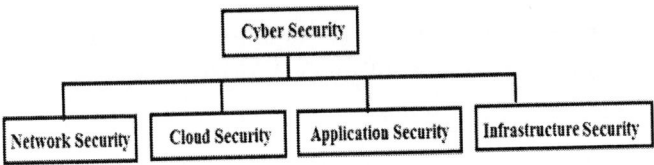

Figure 2. Cyber security domains.

1. *Network Security:* It protects the network from unauthorized access. Many tools are being developed to implement network security framework.
2. *Cloud Security:* Cloud is used by almost all the organizations whether big or large. Since all the important data transfers and storage are done there, it must be protected properly. Cloud providers must use new tools to safeguard their data.
3. *Application Security:* Web application security has become the weakest side. The web pages are morphed and used in a wrong way. But latest tools that are emerging will help the people to guard their pages and other applications from falling in wrong hands.
4. *Infrastructure Security:* Security provided to the pivotal infrastructure (like Emergency, defense, commercial sectors etc.).

1.3. Requirements of Cyber Security

A few basic requirements of cyber security are

a) *People:* Every individual person is responsible for preventing the threats. They must be up-to-date with the solutions for all risks.
b) *Processes:* The processes that are documented must explain duty, management and rules. They must be periodically viewed.

c) *Technology:* The latest technologies are to be installed to minimize the number of cyber threats. It is made sure that the installation of this software does not bring further threats to the computer or any digital device.

1.4. Benefits

Cyber security allows us to deal with the assets correctly and protects them from misuse. It provides a bunch of benefits as such in [4].

- There is always protection for all information and networks.
- Unauthorized access is highly prohibited.
- It shields from a varied set of virus, malware virus, malware, worms and others that affects the entire system.
- Minimizes the possibilities of system or network crash due to attacks.

1.5. Complications

Cyber security also has some dark sides. The few disadvantages [5] are

- It is quite expensive for ordinary people.
- A proper configuration of network software/hardware is required. An incorrect configuration may block the legitimate access.
- It is essential to periodically keep the software updated.
- As security threats are infinite more expertise is required to implement security policies to ensure the security of assets.

2. APPLYING AI FOR CYBER SECURITY

AI is a prominent domain which can be combined with cyber security for implementing superior security policies. Many organizations are employing AI based systems that analyzes the incoming and outgoing network traffic to assist cybersecurity professionals to identify various threats and take necessary actions to resolve them. Without AI, the implementation of cybersecurity tools that learn on their own by analyzing the things would not be possible. To implement this kind of functionality the training datasets must be required. Based on this training dataset new automated AI tools can be developed to enhance the effectiveness of current cybersecurity schemes [8, 10].

We explained how AI can be used to protect organization's assets from various cyberattacks [9].

2.1. AI Based Authentication

Password is a general way of providing authentication which is very fragile in the context of security. Due to this reason, biometric based authentication schemes are used widely. But due to advancements in technology attackers can also compromise the biometric based security schemes [6].

For example: a face recognition system cannot able to detect the same face with different hairstyles. This type of authentication scheme can be compromised by the attacker by getting different images from the social media. By using AI, biometric based authentication can be enhanced and get rid of various difficulties that exist in traditional schemes. AI can be used to create a sophisticated model of the user's face by identifying key correlations and patterns. Apple claims that, with this technology, there's only one-in-a-million chance of fooling the AI and opening the device with another face. The AI based software can also work in different circumstances and support the changes like a new hairstyle, wearing a hat or eyeglass etc.

2.2. Phishing Detection Using AI

It is one of the most widely used cyber-attack that is used by attackers to get personal information of legitimate users. AI based system can able to scan phishing sources and make faster decisions than the human expert can do. AI based software can also be trained to differentiate between fake and legitimate websites [6].

2.3. AI Based Behavioral Analysis

AI based behavioral analysis is a promising way of handling cyber attacks. The usage of ML algorithms can results in a model that can learn and anlayze your behavior by creating behavioral patterns based on how you use your device. It also records and analyzes your way of typing, speed of typing, mouse clicks, surfing, scrolling patterns etc. At any time, if AI identifies unusual behavior that doesn't matches your standard patterns, then it can determine that the activities are done by unauthorized user [6].

2.4. AI Based Malware Detection

Malware detection has been a persistent challenge for cyber security professionals. Traditional malware detection schemes are signature-based, also relies on static and dynamic analysis. Due to enormous growth in malicious code, there is a huge demand for novel malware detection schemes. ML techniques can be employed for malware detection. Most of the research work is done on implementing frameworks for analysis, acquiring static features and classifying malware families. The main weakness of ML-based malware detection systems is that they rely on a virtual environment to analyze samples. This property not only affects the runtime performance but also endangers the whole system since the samples need to be executed. Due to the adaptable behavior of malware, the accurate detection of malware is not possible. So some innovative AI based algorithms must be developed to perform effective malware detection. Irina Baptista et al., proposed an image based malware detection technique that is based on unsupervised learning. This proposed technique gives more accuracy and a better detection rate than the traditional malware detection schemes.

CONCLUSION

In this chapter, we explained how increase in digitization demands the cyber security policies to protect the digital world from various cyberattacks. We also explained the role of AI in implementing various cyber security schemes effectively as demanded by today's digital world. As AI is outperforming its role in cyber security, it is also playing its best in contradictory angles. That means AI is also employed by the attackers to launch various intelligent attacks that are very difficult to detect unless some powerful security policies were developed. AI in the hands of an attacker can do extreme damage and become a stronger threat to cybersecurity. So more and more research must be carried out in this direction to overcome such situations.

REFERENCES

[1] https://digitalguardian.com/blog/whatcyber-security.
[2] https://www.techopedia.com/definition/2387/cybercrime.
[3] https://searchsecurity.techtarget.com/definition/cybersecurity.
[4] http://asmartc.blogspot.com/2015/04/cyber-security-advantages-and_18.html.
[5] https://sites.google.com/site/xinyicyber/the-disadvantages-andadvantages-of-cyber-security.
[6] https://www.entrepreneur.com/article/339509.
[7] Baptista I., Shiaeles, S. and Kolokotronis, N. "A Novel Malware Detection System Based on Machine Learning and Binary Visualization," 2019 *IEEE International Conference on Communications Workshops* (ICC Workshops).
[8] Rajan, H. M. and Dharani S., "Aritificial Intelligence in Cyber Security- AN Investigation," *IRJCS, Issue* 09, Volume 4 (September 2017).
[9] Devakunchari, R., Sourabh and Prabhakar Malik, "A Study of Cyber Security using Machine Learning Techniques," *IJITEE,* Volume 8, Issue 7C2, May 2019.
[10] Arockia Panimalar, S., GiriPai, U. and Salman Khan K., "Artificial Intelligence Techniques for Cyber Security," *IRJET,* Volume 05, Issue 03, March 2018.

In: A Closer Look at Cybersecurity ... ISBN: 978-1-53618-165-4
Editors: Ch. Rupa et al. © 2020 Nova Science Publishers, Inc.

Chapter 7

AN ANALYTICAL APPROACH FOR CHECKING THE PERFORMANCE OF DIFFERENT CLASSIFIERS IN NETWORK OF IDS

N. Raghavendra Sai*
Department of C. S. E., Koneru Lakshmaiah Education Fundation, Guntur, Andhra Pradesh

ABSTRACT

The Internet is forcing organizations into an era of open and trustworthy communications. This openness at a uniform time brings its share of vulnerabilities and issues like monetary losses, injury to name, maintaining the supply of services, protective the non-public and client information and plenty of additional, pushing each enterprise and repair suppliers to want steps to shield their valuable data from intruders, hackers, and insiders. Intrusion Detection System has become the elemental want for flourishing content networking.

---

* Corresponding Author's Email: nallagatlaraghavendra@kluniversity.in.

IDS provides two primary benefits: Visibility and management. It's the mixture of those two edges that build it getable to form and enforce an enterprise security policy to create the non-public electronic network secure [1]. Visibility is that the flexibility to examine and understand the character of the traffic on the network whereas management is that the ability to possess an impression on network traffic as well as access to the network or components therefrom. Visibility is preponderant to deciding and makes it attainable to make a security policy supported quantitative, real-world information. Management is important to social control and makes it attainable to enforce compliance with security policy.

Keywords: IDS, visibility, classification

1. INTRUSION DETECTION ARCHITECTURE

Intrusion Detection System is used to locate every sort of malignant framework action and workstation use that can't be recognized by a standard firewall. It joins organize attacks against fragile organizations, data has driven ambushes on PC applications, have based attacks, for instance, advantage and approvals uplifting, unapproved logins and access to delicate reports, and malware (contaminations, Trojan steeds, and worms). IDS domain unit the most direct fine-grain channel set inside the guaranteed mastermind, chasing down far-prestigious or extraordinary risks in framework development just as audit information recorded by has. The IDS configuration is exhibited as follows.

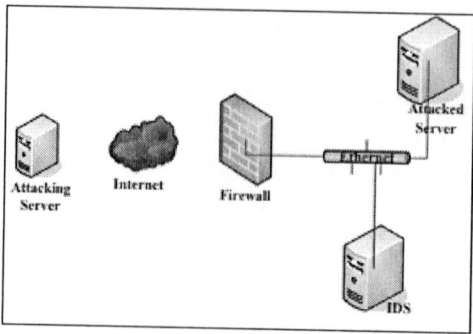

Figure 1. IDS Architecture.

1.1. Data Mining Used in IDS

Information mining is the course toward finding enchanting data in broad documents of information. Basically, more unequivocally, the term intimates the use of unprecedented includes in a system considering sound benchmarks from various solicitations including estimations, man-made scholarly ability, AI, database science, and data recovery [2]. Here region unit some specific things that data dealing with would maybe add to an interference recognizable proof structure:

- Remove run of the mill development from alert data to empower assessment to practice on veritable ambushes.
- Recognize bogus alert generators and "horrendous" sensor marks.
- Find an atypical development that uncovers a real attack.
- Recognize long, consistent models (differing IP addresses, same activity).

Inspirations to use data mining approaches in IDS:

1. It is hard to program IDS using customary programming tongues that require the maltreatment and formalization of learning.
2. The change and dynamic nature of AI make it a proper response to this condition.
3. The state of an IDS and its portrayal task incredibly rely on singular tendencies. What may appear, apparently, to be a scene in one condition might be normal in different conditions. Consequently, the flexibility of PCs to learn draws in them to know somebody's "individual" (or different leveled) propensities, and improve the execution of the IDS, for this specific condition.

1.1.1. Data Mining Techniques for IDS

Information mining strategies assume a key job in IDS. entirely unexpected information preparing methods like arrangement, bunching, affiliation run mining region unit utilized in many cases to store up information concerning interruptions by perceptive and dissecting the system data. The accompanying portrays the diverse information mining methods:

A. *Classification:* Intrusion location technique can be considered as an arrangement issue. It will group each occasion as ordinary or a particular sort of interruption (assault). Its principal objective is to gain from class-marked preparing examples for foreseeing classes of new or already inconspicuous information Instances in the preparation set have names. New information is classed bolstered the training set. Fundamentally, a characterization tree (additionally called a choice tree) is worked to anticipate the class to which a specific occurrence has a place.

B. *Association Rule:* This strategy looks through a regularly happening thing set from a huge dataset. Affiliation rules mining finds a connection between's the attributes. The idea of relationship of lead digging for interruption identification was presented by Lee. This system was at first connected to the alleged market bushel investigation, which goes for discovering regularities in the shopping conduct of clients of grocery stores.

C. *Clustering:* An unsupervised machine learning system for finding designs in unlabeled information. It is utilized to mark information and doles out it into groups where each bunch comprises of individuals that are very comparative. Individuals from various groups will fluctuate from one another. The different grouping approaches are Density-based strategies, Grid-based techniques, Model-based techniques, Partitioning strategies, and Hierarchy strategies.

1.2. Data Mining Algorithms in IDS

The absolute most regularly utilized information mining calculations which have been generally executed in IDS is given underneath.

1.2.1. Decision Trees

The notable machine learning strategies. Choice tree learning utilizes a Decision as a prophetic model that maps perceptions with respect to a thing to ends in regards to the thing's objective worth. Choice tree learning might be a method generally used in information handling. The objective is to shape a model that predicts the value of an objective variable bolstered many information factors. Choice trees have also been utilized for interruption identification. The trees pick the best alternatives for each choice hub all through the improvement of the tree upheld some very much characterized criteria. One such rule is to utilize the information to pick up size relation.

Points of interest:

1. Construction does not require any area information.
2. Can handle high dimensional information.
3. Representation is straightforward.
4. Can ready to process both numerical and clear cut information.

Burdens:

1. Construction does not require any area information.
2. Output trait must be downright.
3. Limited to one yield quality.
4. Decision tree calculations are temperamental
5. The Trees made from numeric informational indexes can be perplexing.

1.2.2. Bayesian System Classifier

A Bayesian system is a strategy that encodes probabilistic connections among factors of intrigue. Bayesian systems represent a new approach to detection and prevention of attacks in PC arranges; the use of Bayesian systems in IDS takes care of the lion's share of issues connected to IDS. This system is at times utilized for interruption identification related to arithmetic plans.

Favorable circumstances:

1. Naive Bayesian classifiers simplify the computations.
2. Exhibit high accuracy and speed when applied to large databases.

Detriments:

1. The assumptions made in class conditional independence.
2. Lack of accessible likelihood information.

1.2.3. K-Nearest Neighbor

The k-closest neighbor calculation (k-NN) is a non-parametric strategy for characterization and relapse that predicts articles' "qualities" or class enrollments in light of the k nearest preparing examples in the feature space. It is a sort of lazy learning where the capacity is just approximated locally and all calculations conceded until order. The k-closest neighbor manages is among the best of all machine learning calculations: relate degree question is surveyed by a dominant part vote of its neighbors, with the thing being allocated to the classification commonest among its k closest neighbors. By and large, it's utilized for interruption location together with connected math plans (irregularity recognition).

Points of interest:

1. Analytically tractable.
2. Simple execution.

3. Use local information, which can yield highly adaptive conduct.
4. Lends itself effortlessly to parallel executions.

Burdens:

1. Large capacity necessities.
2. Highly vulnerable to the scourge of dimensionality.
3. Slow in characterizing test tuples.

1.2.4. Artificial Neural Network

Counterfeit neural systems are computational models propelled by creature focal sensory systems. Neural systems are utilized each in irregularity interruption discovery still as in abuse interruption location [3]. For irregularity interruption recognition, neural systems were sculpturesque to discover the ordinary qualities of framework clients and build up measurably essential varieties from the client's built up to conduct. In abuse interruption recognition the neural system would get information from the system stream and investigate the learning for examples of abuse. A NN for abuse location is actualized in two different ways. The principal approach consolidates the neural system part into partner degree existing or changed the gifted framework. The second appointment utilized the neural system as an independent abuse location framework.

Points of interest:

1. It requires less formal factual preparation.
2. Implicitly able to detect complex nonlinear relationships among ward and Autonomous factors.
3. High resistance for clamour information.
4. Availability of numerous preparation calculations.

Burdens:

1. "Black box" nature.
2. Greater computational weight.
3. Proneness to overfitting.
4. It requires a long preparation time.

1.2.5. Support Vector Machine

Bolster vector machine anticipated as a vital procedure for interruption discovery framework. It is a machine learning algorithmic administer which is used for both classification and regression. Some standard SVMs (Support Vector Machines) which are intense devices for information order, orders two-classification indicates by doling out them one of two disjoint half-spaces in either the higher dimensional element space for nonlinear classifiers and main input space of the problem for linear classifiers.

Points of interest:

1. Highly precise
2. Able to show complex nonlinear choice limits
3. Less prone to overfitting other methods algorithms.

Inconveniences:

1. High algorithmic multifaceted nature and broad memory necessities of the required quadratic writing computer programs are in extensive scale undertakings.
2. The decision of the portion is troublesome.
3. The speed of both in preparing and testing is moderate.

1.2.6. K-Means Clustering

K-Means algorithm is an exhausting partitioned bunching calculation generally utilized in light of its straightforwardness and speed. It utilizes Euclidean separation as the similarity measure. Hard clustering implies that an item in an informational index can have a place with one and just a single group at any given moment. It is a bunch investigation calculation that gatherings things in light of their element [4] esteems into k disjoint groups with the end goal that the things in the same cluster have similar attributes and those in different clusters have diverse qualities. The algorithmic lead is connected to preparing datasets which may contain normal and abnormal traffic without being marked beforehand.

Points of interest:

1. Easy to actualize.
2. High precision and quicker execution when connected for extensive datasets.

Detriments:

1. The likelihood of creating void bunches.
2. Apriority particular in the number of bunches.
3. With a worldwide cluster, it didn't work well. Different initial partitions can result in a few last groups.
4. It does not work well with clusters (in the original data) of Different sizes and Different thicknesses.

1.2.7. Genetic Algorithms

Hereditary calculations were at first presented in the knoll of computational science. From that point onward, they have been sprouted into different fields with a promising outcome [7]. These days the researchers have tried to incorporate this algorithm with IDSs. By, Using the Genetic approach, in 1995 Giordana and Nerih proposed one intrusion detection algorithms called Regal. The REGAL System depends on a dispersed hereditary calculation. Great is one of the ideas learning frameworks that adapt First Order Logic multi-show idea depictions. The learning examples are stored in a relational database that is represented as relational tuples.

Gonzalez and Dasgupta applied a genetic algorithm, although they were examined host-based IDSs, not network-based. They used the algorithmic program just for the Meta-learning step rather than running the algorithm directly on the feature set. It uses the statistical classifiers for labeled vectors. Two-bit binary encoding methodology is used for identifying the abnormality of a particular feature, ranging from normal to abnormal. Chittur used a genetic algorithm with a decision tree. A decision tree is used to represent the data. They have used the high detection rate that reduces the false positive rate. The false-positive prevalence was reduced by utilizing human input in a feedback loop.

Points of Interest:

1. It solves every optimization problem.
2. It solves the problems with multiple solutions
3. Easily transferred to existing models.

Detriments:

1. No global optimum.
2. No constant optimization response time.

1.3. Models

1.3.1. Artificial Neural Network (ANN)

Artificial Neural Network (ANN) is comparatively crude electronic models based on the neural structure of the brain [5]. The brain primarily learns from his expertise. This is natural proof that some issues that are beyond the scope and range of current computers are indeed solvable by small energy efficient packages. This brain modeling is a technical way to develop machine solutions. This new approach to computing also provides a more graceful degradation during system overload than its more habitual counterparts.

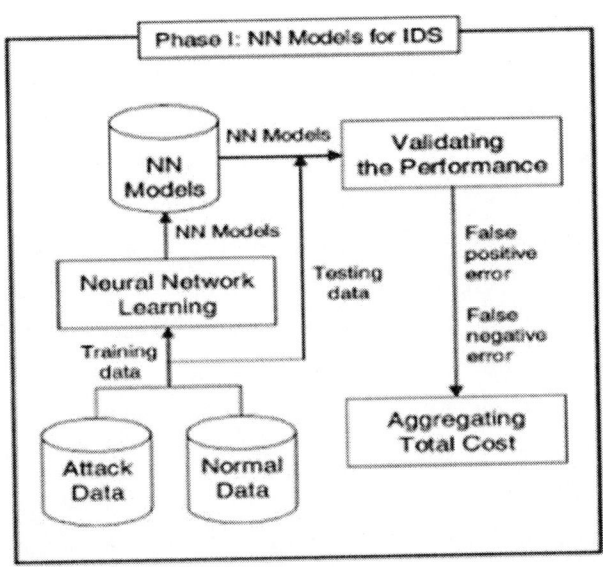

Figure 2. NN Models for IDS.

A neural system is a reticulated gathering of fake neurons that uses a scientific model or computational model for data preparing in view of an association way to deal with the calculation. A neural system couldn't contain space information at the outset; however, it tends to be regulated to settle on choices by mapping model sets of info information into precedent yield vectors and appraisals its weights so it maps each info model vector into the relating yield model vector approx.

1.3.2. Support Vector Machines (SVM)

The SVM approach changes over data into a component territory F that sometimes features a mammoth measurement. This is intriguing to take note of that SVM speculation relies upon the geometrical properties of the directed information, not on the measurements of the information space [6].

1.3.3. Multivariate Adaptive Regression Splines (MARS)

Splines can be considered as an inventive scientific process for confused, hard bend illustrations and capacity uncertain. The MARS model could be a relapse show exploitation fundamental capacities as indicators as opposed to fact duplicate data. The essential capacity convert makes it conceivable to specifically clear out specific districts of a variable by making them zero, and enables MARS to center around specific sub-locales of the record [8]. It exceeds expectations at discovering ideal variable changes and collaborations, and the refined association that dependably covers up in high-dimensional data.

1.3.4. Bayesian Thinking

Bayesian thinking hypothesis thinking is considered here a general expression for an assortment of methods that endeavor the mathematician hypothesis to damage vulnerability.

> "Bayesian reasoning gives a probabilistic method to manage steady thinking. it helped the idea that the amounts of intrigue unit of measurement dominate incidentally disseminations that ideal options could likewise be made by thinking in regards to these probabilities at the part of found data [9]." there's a different change of executions of hypothesis thinking in IDSs.

1.3.4.1. Bayesian Systems

Starting late, speculation frameworks are utilized inside the calling procedure for crossbreed structures [10]. Speculation frameworks give an additional unnoticeable method for managing this differentiated and an fight that the lion's offer cross breed structures secure high forewarning rates because of direct approaches to manage to join the yields of the frameworks inside the call part. They propose a blend that has based peculiarity acknowledgment system involving area methodology: examining string length, character transport, and structure, and perceiving learned tokens, inside which a theory compose is used to pick an authoritative yield arrange.

The system was real on the DARPA99 dataset, differentiated, and a straightforward edge-based approach [11]. Every technique (Bayesian and edge) got vague yields from the area methods. With 100 percent honest to goodness positives, the edge-based generally approach causes fill in as a couple of false encouraging points in light of the speculation orchestrate.

Vague revelation techniques are grasped, and that they secure improved distinguishing proof rates. It conjointly rehearse PC gear stack, since the IDS shouldn't take up too much a couple of advantages since it would keep the customer from maltreatment the expeditiously. In their preliminaries, the PC hardware stack remained about low. All through weight tests, the rising in PC hardware stack was among two-hundredths on the ordinary.

1.3.5. Naïve Bayes

Innocent Bayes (NB) could in like manner be an enhanced variation of speculation frameworks, [12] which give machine learning limits there are two specific drawbacks of theoretical frameworks, particularly the need for from the prior data concerning the issue to see changes, which the procedure is computationally extravagant. For the past, it's plausible to expel changes from training learning, if reachable that is refined with NB. Regardless, NB will acknowledge that each one of the decisions inside the data are autonomous of every choice ,that is that the reason Associate in apply speculation frameworks to data interference ID instead of NB. Withal, NB (utilized as a classifier) has been viably associated with orchestrating based intrusion ID by a couple of researchers.

Ben Amor et al. drove a correct examination of the KDD Cup '99 data set, an examination of the execution of NB, and a Decision Tree (DT). The DT obtains an improved accuracy (92.28% differentiated and ninety 1.47%), regardless, NB gets higher area rates on the three minor classes one, unmistakably curious, U2R, and R2L intrusions. most on a very basic level, the DT recognizes basically 0.52% R2L intrusions however NB recognizes 7.11%.

Comparable acknowledgments are made by Panda and Patra, as they separate NB and Associate in Nursing ANN. ANNs and disarray tremens are lopsided towards the key class and, thusly, are in danger of playing out even more awful inside the minor class(es). Accordingly, this could be viewed as something to be keen to about the NB, giving the FPR doesn't wind up being excessively high.

Observations like those made by mount god and Panda and Patra as said on high of, animate possible hybridizations of systems. For instance, Benfer cap and Taiba, equivalently to mount god, normally see that NB is increasingly important at examining two or three obstructions than a DT [13]. They underline an issue with bogus negative rates that lead them to the union of a mutt course of action of variety from the standard ID and abuse territory, allowing the characteristic disclosure module to hurt the standard development. Thames River completed an undifferentiated from half and half illustrate, setting up a Self-Organizing Map (SOM) on standard models, that limits as a central level interruption identifier. At the subsequent level, NB joins its strategy thereto of the Kyrgyzstani money related unit. This half and half structure semiconductor diodes to raised solicitation rates than misuse NB alone.

CONCLUSION

This chapter explains about the analytical Approach for Checking the Performance of Different Classifiers in Networks for IDS. We have discussed in this chapter about various data mining techniques and algorithms used in IDS. It is determined that the Network system has to be secured from all types of attacks. Most of the Data mining techniques for IDS accessible in the writing demonstrate one of a kind inclinations for identifying a specific class of assault with enhanced precision while performing respectably for alternate classes of assaults.

- The Chapter presents the Intrusion Detection Architecture and Data mining used in IDS.
- Many research works are carried out using predictive models like Decision trees, SVM, Fuzzy logic, Bayesian Networks, K-nearest Neighbour, K-means clustering, genetic algorithms advantages, and disadvantages are presented in this chapter.
- In most researches, the detection rate alone was taken as the performance metrics for the effective evaluation of IDS which is not enough. For efficient IDS there should be a hybrid combination of two or more classifiers which gives better results.
- Most of the IDS generate a model by almost predicting the majority class. This results in a higher error rate for the minority class than the Majority class.

REFERENCES

[1] Bishop, C.: Novelty detection and neural network validation. *IEEE Proceedings on Vision, Image and Signal Processing, Special Issue on Applications of Neural Networks* 141(4), 217–222 (1994).

[2] Cortes C. and V. Vapnik, Support-Vector Networks, *Machine Learning*, 20(3):273-297, September 1995.

[3] An, G. 1996. The effects of adding noise during back propagation training on a generalization performance. *Neural Computation*, 8, 643–674. ISSN 0899-7667.

[4] Ritter, G., Gallegos, M.: Outliers in statistical pattern recognition and an application to automatic chromosome classification. *Pattern Recognition Letters* 18, 525–539 (1997).

[5] Cannady, J. "Artificial Neural Networks for Misuse Detection," *National Information Systems Security Conference*, 1998.

[6] Roesch Martin, 1999. Snort–lightweight intrusion detection for networks, *13th Systems Administration Conference* (LISA), pages 229–238.

[7] Alba and J. M. Troya. 1999. A survey of parallel distributed genetic algorithms. *Complexity*, 4, 31–52. ISSN 1076-2787.

[8] Lee, W. A Data *Mining Framework for Constructing Features and Models for Intrusion Detection Systems.* PhD. thesis, Columbia University, 1999.

[9] Japkowicz, N.: *Concept-Learning in the absence of counter examples: An auto association-based approach to classification.* PhD. thesis, New Brunswick Rutgers, The State University of New Jersey (1999).

[10] Lee, Wenke, Salvatore J. Stolfo, and Kui. Mok. A data mining framework for building intrusion detection models. Security and Privacy, 1999. *Proceedings of the 1999 IEEE Symposium on. IEEE,* 1999.

[11] Angeline, P. J. *Evolutionary Computation 1: Basic Algorithms and Operators, chapter Parse trees,* pages155–159. Institute of Physics Publishing, 2000.

[12] Pfahringer, Bernhard, Winning the KDD99 Classification Cup: Bagged Boosting, *ACMSIGKDD Explorations Newsletter*, Volume 1, Issue2, p. 65-66 January 2000.

[13] Levin, Itzhak, KDD-99 Classifier Learning Contest LL Soft's Results Overview, *ACM SIGKDD Explorations Newsletter*, Volume 1, Issue 2, p. 67-75January 2000.

In: A Closer Look at Cybersecurity ... ISBN: 978-1-53618-165-4
Editors: Ch. Rupa et al. © 2020 Nova Science Publishers, Inc.

Chapter 8

SMART IOT DEVICE FOR WOMEN SAFETY

Chattu Padmini, Gade Brahma Reddy,
Kunapareddy Chaitanya Sai, Chundru Sowmya Lalitha
and Bode Siri Krishna*

Computer Science and Engineering,
Dhanekula Institute of Engineering and Technology,
Vijayawada, Andhra Pradesh, India

ABSTRACT

At present women safety is a major issue in our country. Every day we hear about the news of women abuse & harassment. Most of the people are ready to save women when they hear about women harassment. So we are creating an IoT device [2] which can ensure safety to women with people's help. The people who are ready to save a woman/girl can register t+-hemselves to a website. The registered details are stored in a database. Our proposed system has a force sensor which can be triggered by women when they encounter any problem. The GPS module gets the current location of women. When a force sensor is

---

* Corresponding Author's Email: getmini2004@gmail.com.

triggered the victim's location is sent to registered people, parents, and police. We are running the entire system by using Raspberry Pi. We used Python programming language as an intermediate between sensors and hardware.

Keywords: women safety, IoT, raspberry Pi, force sensor, GPS, database

1. INTRODUCTION

Now-a-days Internet of Things is connected with our daily activities and it has become a part of our lives. With the advancement of sensor technology, availability of internet connected devices makes IoT devices to act smart devices [2] in emergency situations without human intervention. IoT is used in almost every field such as sensing, Networking, Robotics. As technology advances IoT [3] will become a part of our day to day life.

Through IoT Humans save time, resources and human power by providing the real time services without any intervention of humans.

At present women are equal with men in every aspect of work. Women's contribution to the development of our nation is immense. But we are living in a society that can't ensure safety to women. The crimes against women are increasing abruptly. This paper proposes an alert based system that is able to track the present location of women. The system sends location to registered people [who pledged for women safety, police and parents. Our system provides a smart solution [1] that can definitely ensure safety to women.

2. METHODS

2.1. Related Works

Many applications or gadgets [6] have been designed for ensuring safety to women but they can't provide a complete solution to the problem. Some of them are: One system sends the current location of women to parents and police stations when the panic button is pressed. Some other systems send location to police when their heart beat increases through heart beat sensor. Many other researchers did a lot of research work for tracking systems; it was a basic system to send location of the user by using GSM. Other IoT based devices provide the current location of women on a web server. Other IoT devices use GPS [5] and pressure switches. Whenever a switch is pressed the current location is sent to emergency contacts. The main drawbacks with the current devices are the medical related sensors are not giving accurate results. Whenever a woman sees any accident then heartbeat rises then location is sent to parents even if there is no problem. Suppose if the victim is far away from the police station and parents then they can't reach the location within time. By perceiving the news of women abuse and harassment many people feel that if they were at the location they can readily save the girl. So we proposed an idea that can definitely ensure safety to women by the people who are ready to save the woman. We developed a Raspberry Pi system for the first time which provides location of victims to all the registered people.

2.2. Proposed Methodology

We created an IoT device that can definitely ensure safety to women. If a woman feels any problem she can just press the force sensor then the Raspberry Pi system sends the current location of women to all the registered people, parents & police. The components present in our system are Raspberry Pi, Force Sensor, AD Converter, GPS, Web Application, SMS Gateway, and Database. The block diagram is shown in Figure 1.

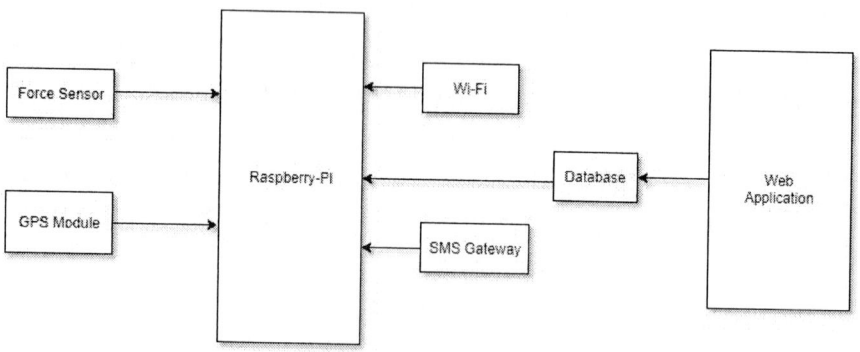

Figure 1. Block diagram.

2.2.1. Hardware Components

2.2.1.1. Raspberry Pi

Raspberry is a small sized computer that can be connected to a display unit, it can be either a computer monitor or projector. It can perform anything that you expect from a desktop computer to do.

2.2.1.2. GPS

GPS [5] is an navigation based system that is used to determine the current position of an object in terms of latitude and longitude. There are 24 satellites deployed in space which surrounds the earth. This satellite broadcasts the position of an object. GPS uses a triangulation process to obtain the exact position of an object. The GPS module is connected to Raspberry Pi through GPIO pins.

2.2.1.3. Force Sensor

The Force Sensor material resistance varies when any force or stress is applied on it. The conductive polymer is responsible for changing the resistance inside the material. The Force sensor is connected to a digital convertor which in turn the digital converter is connected to Raspberry Pi GPIO pins.

2.2.1.4. AD Convertor

Basically the input from the force sensor is an analog signal. So in order to convert it into digital signal we use Analog to Digital converter. It takes Analog signal as input from force sensor and sends digital signal as output to Raspberry Pi.

2.2.2. Software Components

2.2.2.1. Web Server

UwAmp is a free web server that can be installed on a local PC. UmAmp has the following components such as Apache, MySql, PHP and SQLite. We have to start the server if we want to work. After starting the web server we can add any web pages. The local database stores the details of the registered people.

2.2.2.2. SMS Gateway

SMS Gateway is used to dispatch multiple messages to several people from a web browser. It can also provide international messaging service gateway with roaming facility.

2.2.2.3. Python

Python programming language is used as an interface between Raspberry Pi, Sensors and Database. Python is a flexible programming language with short code and it has multiple libraries. The interaction with Sensors and Raspberry Pi is easy with python programming language.

2.3. Procedure

Whenever the Raspberry Pi system is connected to a power source, the Operating system gets loaded with a green signal blinking on it. Then all the connected components are initialized. The Flowchart of our proposed system is furnished in Figure 2.

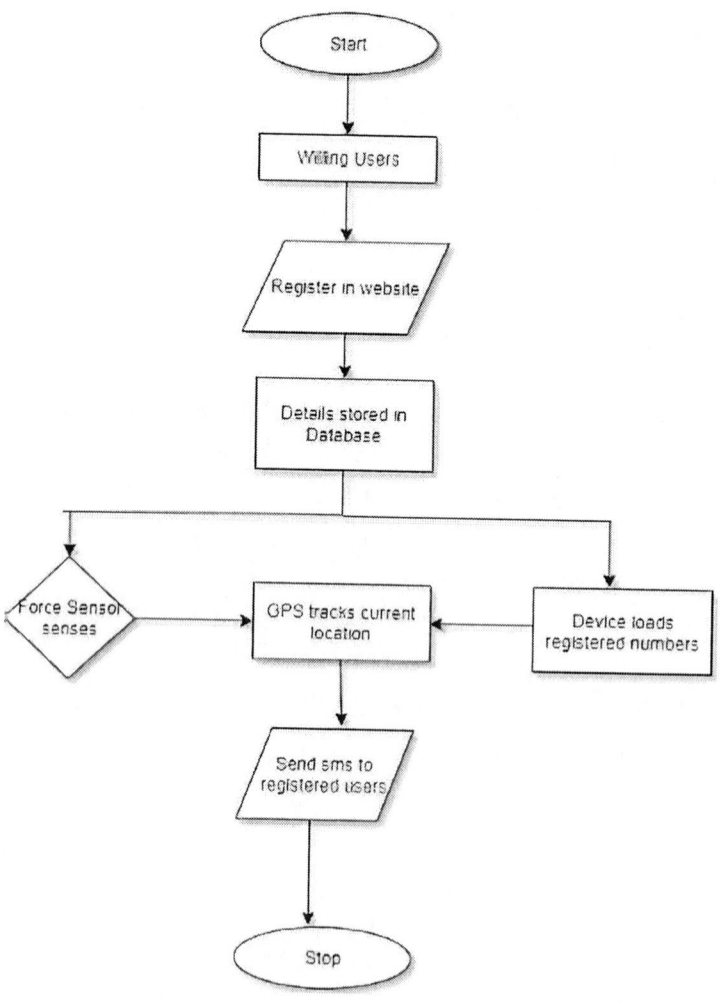

Figure 2. Flowchart.

2.4. Explanation

Step 1: The users who are willing to help women can readily register themselves to a website by providing their details. The details are stored in a database.

Step 2: Whenever a woman feels any problem she can just press the force sensor.

Step 3: The input from the force sensor is read into an AD converter there after the signal is transferred to the Raspberry Pi system.

Step 4: The Raspberry Pi system gets the registered phone numbers from the database.

Step 5: The GPS module gets the current location of the victim when it is triggered by the Raspberry Pi system.

Step 6: Finally the SMS Gateway sends the location of the victim to all the registered people, police & parents.

3. RESULTS

By using VNC Viewer we can affix Raspberry Pi remotely. We have to provide the IP address of Raspberry Pi to VNC Viewer. From VNC Viewer we can perform any operations on Raspberry Pi. Whenever the force sensor is activated then it sends an alternative signal to the AD converter, the AD converter sends a digital signal to Raspberry Pi. When there is an input signal from an AD converter the system gets the location from the GPS module. When program is executing the current location link is sent to sms gateway. It is shown in Figure 3.

```
>>> %Run siws.py
    16.5995 49.6673
    http://maps.google.com/?q=16.5995,49.6673
    Sent.c.
```

Figure 3. Sending current location.

3.1. SMS Output

The Raspberry Pi system gets the Contact numbers of all registered persons; thereafter it sends the current location of victim to registered numbers. The SMS to registered people is shown in Figure 4.

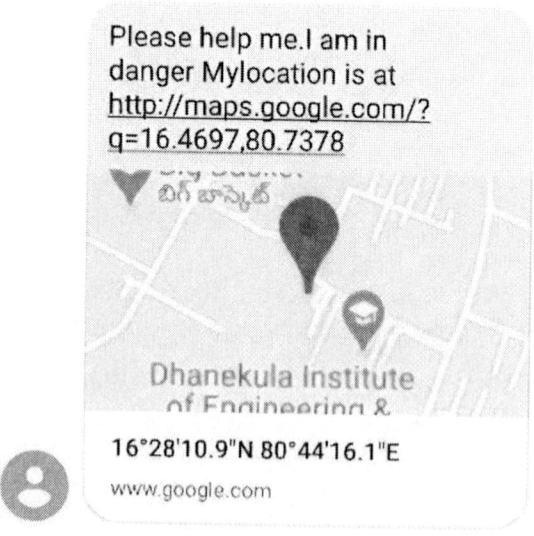

Figure 4. SMS to all registered contacts. Smart IoT Device for Women Safety.

CONCLUSION

This paper mainly focuses on providing safety to women. Our main theme is to ensure safety for every woman so that they can do their work at any time without fear. So "Smart IoT Device for Women Safety" [4] is set up for preventing threats to women in our society. It works on, when the force sensor gets activated by the women then the signals are transmitted to Raspberry Pi, then it collects the registered user's data and sends an alert message through SMS gateway along with the location using GPS. The users can readily save the victim.

REFERENCES

[1] Jesudoss A., Nikhila Y., Smart solution for women safety using IoT in *International Journal of Pure and Mathematics,* Volume 119 No.12, 2018.

[2] Krishna Priyanka S., Tatavarthi Tarun, IoT for women safety in *International Journal of Advanced Research in Science and Engineering,* Vol.No.6, special issue(01), September 2017, BVCNSCS 2017.

[3] Budebhai M., IoT Based Child and Women Safety, *International Journal of Computer Science and Mobile Computing,* vol.7, Issue.8, August 2018.

[4] Harikiran G. C., Smart security solution for women based on Internet of Things published in *International Conference on Electrical, Electronics and Optimization Techniques,* March 2016.

[5] Deepali, IoT Based Unified Approach for Women and Children Security using Wireless and GPS, *International Journal of Advanced Research in Computer Engineering & Technology,* volume 5, Issue 8, August 2016.

[6] Kavya, IoT Based Women's Safety Gadget in *International Journal of Innovative Research in Science, Engineering and Technology,* volume 7, March 2018.

About the Editors

Ch. Rupa
Professor
Department of C.S.E, V.R Siddhartha Engineering College,
Vijayawada, Andhra Pradesh, India

Dr. Ch. Rupa is presently working as Professor in the department of C.S.E, V.R Siddhartha Engineering College, India. She is having more than 15 Years of rich teaching and research experience. Her areas of interest are Information Security, Blockchain Technology, Applied Security with IoT, Image Processing, Data Analytics etc. She published her research work in many repudiated national/international journals and also designated as keynote speaker in various national/international conferences which are indexed by SCI/SCOPUS. She also filed and published many patents in the domain of security. For all these eminent contributions she received many national and international awards.

About the Editors

Mohammad Sirajuddin

Assistant Professor
Department of C.S.E, K.L.E.F (Deemed to be University),
Vaddeswaram, Guntur, Andhra Pradesh, India

Mohammmad Sirajuddin is presently working as Assistant Professor in the department of C.S.E, K.L.E.F, India. He is doing his PhD in the area of Wireless Networks & Security. His areas of interest are Computer Networks, Information Security, Blockchain Technology and Bigdata Analytics.

INDEX

A

abuse, 89, 91
access, 2, 36, 40, 43, 44, 45, 46, 48, 50, 54, 65, 66, 67, 68
advancement, 23, 63, 69, 90
adversary, 1, 2
affine cipher, 3, 4, 5, 7, 8
AI based cyber security, 64
algorithm(s), 2, 3, 4, 5, 9, 10, 11, 13, 14, 15, 16, 17, 18, 19, 21, 22, 24, 28, 29, 30, 31, 35, 70, 71, 77, 80, 81
analogy, 1
analysis, vii, 1, 3, 10, 12, 13, 16, 20, 22, 26, 28, 35, 40, 45, 46, 47, 48, 49, 62, 70
architecture, 17, 48, 50, 74
artifical neural network (ANN), 82
artificial, 26, 28, 32, 72, 79, 82
artificial intelligence (AI), vii, 21, 28, 32, 63, 64, 69, 70, 71, 72
attacker, 10, 11, 12, 14, 16, 27, 37, 40, 42, 45, 66, 69, 71
attacks, vii, 1, 9, 10, 13, 14, 16, 17, 18, 19, 42, 43, 45, 46, 64, 66, 68, 70, 71
authentication, 17, 69
automate, 25, 26, 28
automation, 28

B

Bayesian, 78, 84
behavioral, 70
benefits, 15, 68
birthday attack, 14
block ciphers, 10, 22, 24, 33

C

channel, 4, 12, 13, 16, 17, 45
classification, 74
classifiers, 73, 78
clustering, 80
complications, 68
components, 64, 92, 93, 94
confidentiality, 4, 5, 64
configuration, 49, 62, 68
conquer, 15
convertor, 93
correlation(s), 15, 19, 69

Index

cryptanalysis, vii, 1, 2, 3, 4, 7, 8, 9, 10, 11, 16, 18, 19, 21, 22, 23, 24, 25, 26, 27, 28, 29, 30, 31, 32, 33, 35
cryptanalyst, 2, 3, 4, 7, 26, 29, 30
cryptography, 2, 9, 10, 13, 17, 22, 31, 32
cyber security, 63, 64, 65, 67, 68, 69, 70, 71, 72
cyber-attack, 70
cybersecurity, 69, 71, 72

D

data analysis, 26
data mining, vii, 75
database, 19, 89, 90, 92, 93, 95
detection, 70, 72, 74
detection system, 71
digitization, 63, 64, 66, 71
DNA, 16, 21, 22, 30, 31, 32
DNA computing, 21, 22, 31
domains, 22, 28, 66, 67

E

encryption, 2, 3, 4, 8, 14, 15, 16, 18, 22, 29, 35
evolution, vii, 13, 18, 21
execution, 81
exploitation, 37, 43

F

force, 7, 13, 17, 18, 26, 33, 89, 90, 91, 93, 95, 97
force sensor, 89, 90, 91, 93, 95, 97
functioning, 35, 47, 50, 55, 65

G

gaining, 38, 42, 43, 45, 46

genetic, 81
glitch, 9
GPS, 89, 90, 91, 92, 95, 97

H

harassment, 89, 91
hardware, 16, 17, 45, 68, 90, 92
host, 40, 48, 49, 50, 55, 57, 58, 61, 62

I

infrastructure, 30, 36, 45, 67
input signal, 95
installation, 51, 52, 54, 68
intelligence, 38, 39
intelligence gathering, 39
interface, 54, 93
intervention, 90
intrusion, vii, 74
intrusion detection system (IDS), vii, 73, 74, 75, 76, 77, 83, 84
IoT, vii, 89, 90, 91, 96, 97
IP address, 39, 40, 56, 95

K

K-Means, 80

M

machine, 22, 24, 25, 28, 29, 32, 44, 64, 72, 80
machine learning, 22, 24, 25, 28, 29
maintaining, 38, 44
malleability, 14
malware, 65, 66, 68, 70, 72
mapping, 23
media, 16, 19, 69
memory, 45, 80

messages, 12, 14, 24, 93
methodology, 35, 91
models, 30, 82, 83
multivariate adaptive regression splines (MARS), 84

N

Naïve Bayes, 85
neighbor, 78
Nessus tool, 36, 47, 49, 50, 51, 52
network, 19, 24, 26, 27, 29, 30, 36, 39, 40, 42, 44, 47, 48, 49, 50, 55, 56, 61, 62, 67, 68, 69, 73, 79, 82
networking, 40, 44
neural, 26, 27, 29, 32, 79, 82
neural network, 26, 27, 29
Nmap, 36, 42, 45, 49, 62

O

operations, 17, 23, 95
output, 23, 27, 29, 77, 93, 96

P

parameters, 2, 3, 4, 8
password, 2, 17
phishing, 44, 46, 65, 70
plaintext, 2, 3, 5, 7, 11, 12, 14, 23, 27, 28, 29
problem-solving, 15
programming, 90, 93
protection, 2, 35, 40, 64, 68

Q

quantum computer, 18
quantum computing, 31

R

raspberry Pi, 90, 91, 92, 93, 94, 95, 96, 97
reconnaissance, 38, 39, 41, 46
reporting, 38, 46, 47
requirement(s), 36, 44, 46, 51, 65, 67
researchers, 22, 91
resources, 24, 43, 90
response time, 82

S

safety, 89, 90, 91, 96, 97
SANS, 32
scanning, 38, 40, 41, 42, 43, 45, 48, 50
secure communication, 22
security, vii, 12, 16, 19, 21, 22, 23, 24, 28, 30, 32, 35, 36, 38, 42, 46, 47, 48, 49, 50, 62, 63, 64, 65, 66, 67, 68, 69, 70, 71, 72, 73, 74, 75, 76, 77, 83, 97
security threats, 63, 68
sensitive data, 1, 36, 46, 48, 49, 50, 62
sensor(s), 89, 90, 91, 93, 95, 97
servers, 39, 40, 41, 42, 43
software, 40, 45, 48, 66, 68, 70
solution, 9, 36, 49, 62, 90, 91, 97
strategy, 16, 27
subdomains, 39
support vector machines (SVM), 83
system, 9, 10, 11, 12, 13, 14, 16, 17, 24, 28, 33, 35, 36, 37, 40, 41, 42, 43, 44, 45, 46, 48, 49, 50, 51, 62, 65, 68, 69, 70, 71, 72, 78, 89, 90, 91, 92, 94, 95, 96

T

techniques, vii, 2, 9, 11, 21, 22, 28, 29, 31, 32, 35, 40, 41, 49, 62, 64, 71, 72, 76, 97
technologies, vii, 64, 68
technology, 28, 63, 64, 69, 90

testing, vii, 35, 36, 38, 46, 48, 80
thinking, 84
threats, 44, 45, 65, 67, 68, 69, 97

V

vector, 80
visibility, 74
VoIP, 66
vulnerability, vii, 8, 9, 35, 36, 40, 41, 42, 43, 45, 47, 49, 50, 51, 58, 59, 60, 61, 62, 84

vulnerability assessment, vii, 35, 36, 47, 49, 62

W

weakness, 7, 8, 15, 26, 27, 28, 29, 31, 40, 47, 50, 71
web servier, 39, 42, 91, 93
websites, 42, 65, 70
women safety, 89, 90, 97
worms, 68